WHERE MEN ONLY DARE TO GO

WHERE MEN ONLY DARE TO GO

OR THE

STORY OF A BOY COMPANY,

C.S.A.

ROYALL W. FIGG

UPDATED EDITION

With a Foreword by Robert K. Krick

LOUISIANA STATE UNIVERSITY PRESS

Baton Rouge

Originally published as *"Where Men Only Dare to Go!"* or
The Story of a Boy Company (C.S.A.) in hardcover by Whittet & Shepperson, 1885
Louisiana Paperback Edition, 2008
Foreword and index copyright © 2008 by Louisiana State University Press

FIRST PRINTING

Library of Congress Cataloging-in-Publication Data

Figg, Royall W.
    Where men only dare to go, or, The story of a boy company, C.S.A. / Royall W. Figg ;
with a foreword by Robert K. Krick. — Updated ed.
        p. cm.
    Includes index.
    Originally published: Richmond : Whittet & Shepperson, 1885.
    ISBN 978-0-8071-3378-1 (paper : alk. paper) 1. Figg, Royall W. 2. Confederate
States of America. Army. Virginia Artillery. Parker's Battery. 3. Soldiers—Confederate
States of America—Biography. 4. Soldiers—Virginia—Biography. 5. Virginia—
History—Civil War, 1861–1865—Personal narratives. 6. United States—History—Civil
War, 1861–1865—Personal narratives, Confederate. 7. Virginia—History—Civil
War, 1861–1865—Regimental histories. 8. United States—History—Civil War,
1861–1865—Regimental histories. 9. Virginia—History—Civil War, 1861–1865—Ar-
tillery operations. 10. United States—History—Civil War, 1861–1865—Artillery opera-
tions. I. Title. II. Title: Where men only dare to go. III. Title: Story of a boy company,
C.S.A.
    E581.8.P2F54 2008
    973.7'82—dc22

                                                                    2008029899

The paper in this book meets the guidelines for permanence and durability of the Commit-
tee on Production Guidelines for Book Longevity of the Council on Library Resources.♾

DEDICATION.

IN

MEMORY

OF

THE DEAD

OF

THE PARKER BATTERY,

AND OF

THE BATTALION

SUCCESSIVELY

COMMANDED BY

KEMPER,

LEE, ALEXANDER,

AND

HUGER.

1862—1865.

CONTENTS

FOREWORD

J. Thompson Brown, the last commander of Parker's Virginia Battery, described Royal W. Figg as "a fair representative of our Company, an intelligent fairly educated boy. . . . He was a truthful and Christian gentleman. . . . I believe what he says, as no man could doubt Royal W. Figg's statement."[1] The content of Figg's classic memoir of Confederate service, *Where Men Only Dare to Go; or the Story of a Boy Company, C.S.A.*, confirms Lieutenant Brown's analysis. The narrative contains plenty of piety and clear signs of intelligence and erudition, and under comparison with other sources its contents stand up as accurate to a gratifying extent.

The imminent prospect of a national conscription act prompted creation of numerous new Confederate volunteer companies in the late winter of 1861–62. Most of them attracted young men eager to avoid the ignominy of being drafted. William W. Parker, a much-loved physician in Richmond, announced his plans to form an artillery company with special emphasis on youthful volunteers. His medical background suggested an ideal leader for youngsters going to war, and Parker had the benefit of experience in 1861 with the 15th Virginia Infantry, including participation in the famous early clash at Big Bethel. The "Boy Company" that he recruited served with high distinction through three years of steady fighting.[2]

Parker began recruiting, based in his medical office, on March 1, 1862. Royal Figg joined the doctor-captain's nascent organization in Richmond as a charter member at the battery's initial muster on March 14, held at Old Market Hall. The enlistment documents and a later descriptive list paint a picture of the young man: twenty years old, residing in Richmond, brown hair, blue eyes, five feet eight inches tall. The 1860 Richmond directory shows Figg working as a printer for W. H. Clemmitt and boarding on 23rd between N and O streets.[3]

Although he did not mention it in his subsequent book, Figg already had two months of soldiering experience before he signed Captain Parker's roll. He had entered Confederate service with the "Richmond Light Guard" on August 20, 1861, when that company mustered in as Company H, 60th Virginia Infantry. The other companies of the 60th came from southwestern Virginia, and the regiment deployed there, far removed from the homes and interests of the Light Guard men. The exile from home did not affect Royal Figg for long; he was discharged for disability on October 24, barely two months after joining. He left the regiment after a promotion to corporal, but owing to the Confederate States government the price of a cap, blanket, pants, socks, and shoes.[4]

Surviving official documents verify Figg's steady presence through the war service of Parker's Battery, which he described so vividly and in such detail in *Where Men Only Dare to Go*. Fourteen bimonthly muster rolls for Parker's Battery survive at the National Archives. Figg was marked present on each of them without fail from March 1862 to February 1865—an unusually devoted record. Obviously, either whatever disability had exempted him from service in October 1861 had vanished, or Figg overcame the handicap. During the summer of 1862 he served on detail as orderly to Major Delaware Kemper, an artillery officer superior to Captain Parker. That temporary role certainly did not decrease Figg's exposure to events, and probably increased his access to useful information.[5]

Private Figg apparently spelled his given name, randomly rendered either Royal or Royall in various sources, as "Royal" during the war. His service record contains nineteen documents. Six of them use only "R. W."; four of them spell the first name "Royall"; nine of them spell it "Royal." Three of the four that use "Royall," however, are slips copied from Northern prison documents. All but one of the Confederate slips that use the full name spell it "Royal." Figg's record jacket from his brief interlude in the 60th Virginia also uses "Royal."[6]

Pinning down Figg's middle name proved more difficult than the first name. In fact it cannot be stipulated with any certainty. In a book published last year that mentions Figg's work, I tentatively used Washington for his second given name, based on one of the ubiquitous Mormon Web sites on the Internet. That Web entry subsequently was dismantled. A better estimate than Washington probably would be Wright: Royal's father was Robert Wright Figg, and his grandmother was Sarah Francis Wright.[7]

Because he chose to publish his book anonymously, its title

page does not spell "Royal" at all. It calls the author only "an ex-boy." Occasionally in the narrative Figg refers to himself by the pseudonym "Cannon." In an earlier publication discussed in the next paragraph—a source that sheds considerable light on Figg's production of *Where Men Only Dare to Go*—the young veteran called himself "Number Three," an obvious allusion to his position on a Parker's Battery gun crew. Royal Figg evidently embraced the Victorian-era precept that preferred anonymity in public forums.

An obscure but important early first-person narrative about Parker's Battery came to my attention in the late 1980s. As I completed a heavily revised book-length history of the battery, *Parker's Virginia Battery*, published initially in 1975, I came across a very early periodical that published monthly installments about the unit, written by an anonymous veteran. I cited the new find in the bibliography of the revised 1989 edition as a guide for future researchers; but with production already under way by the publisher, I did not have time to use the articles' contents in any detail.[8]

The arcane source appeared during 1871 and 1872 in a monthly periodical, *The Old Dominion*, which at times bore the subtitle *A Monthly Magazine of Literature, Science and Art.* Some numbers added to the title, tellingly, . . . *and Virginia Historical Register.* In 1871, a veteran of the battery, writing under the pseudonym "Number Three," launched a long-running series of articles. "Reminiscences of Parker's Battery" appeared serially for a whole year in *The Old Dominion.*

Examination of the narrative by "Number Three" makes

unmistakable the author's identity: Royal W. Figg wrote the *Old Dominion* articles. They obviously served as a first venture in the direction of what became, thirteen years later, his classic book, reprinted here. In the May 1871 *Old Dominion* article (vol. 5, no. 5: 278): "Rain! rain! rain! How it poured for days, and made the red Culpeper mud almost as slippery as ice." The same words show up on page 77 of *Where Men Only Dare to Go* with the sole exception of an exclamation point after "ice!" The first variation in language turns up in the thirty-third word in that paragraph. Some passages display a bit more revision, but never enough to obscure the obvious parallels.

From a purely historiographical perspective, the 1871–72 articles strengthen Figg's claims to veracity. That it was written only a few years after the war gives extra credence to the 1885 book, and 1885 actually predates the vast majority of classic Confederate memoirs, published only gradually as the prostrate South regained some economic currency.

Royal Figg's appearance in print in 1871–72, however, substantially deflates a popular story that long has given *Where Men Only Dare to Go* a special kind of cachet, or at least an unusual asterisk next to its listings. In 1950, the nationally syndicated newspaper feature "Ripley's Believe It or Not" reported that Figg's book enjoyed a unique distinction. It was, Ripley claimed, the only book ever composed by an author directly into type, without having first been written as a manuscript. Figg worked in the pressroom for the distinguished Richmond printer and publisher Whittet & Shepperson and supposedly, without benefit of a written manuscript, entered his recollections directly into the type from which the book was printed.

Ripley's researchers had ample grounds for the story, which had gained universal acceptance among knowledgeable Richmonders. Figg's commanding officer reported the fact emphatically in a postwar letter. The author's two surviving nephews verified the story in 1974. The Richmond *News Leader* recalled the event in a 1939 editorial that cited the distinguished local historian, Herbert T. Ezekiel. Veterans' copies of the book, inscribed with the story about its composition, survive to this day. Most impressively, the son of the man who owned and operated Whittet & Shepperson in 1885 repeated the story to me, buttressed by a further account of it from his father to an old-time employee.[9]

The 1871–72 *Old Dominion* articles make abundantly clear the fact that Figg had at least a portion of his book already in hand, in nearly final form, when he began to set the type in 1885 for *Where Men Only Dare to Go.* No doubt he made revisions as he composed type for the book, and he obviously added further material. Some of the gloss comes off the novelty, though, under the light shed by the new information.

Whenever and however the component parts of Figg's narrative came together, their sum total makes a shining contribution to the literature of the Army of Northern Virginia. His subject deserved the attention. Parker's company of young gunners belonged to a battalion that surely stood with the foremost artillery in the army. A succession of uncommonly bright and energetic officers led the battalion: Stephen Dill Lee, who went on to become a lieutenant

general; Edward Porter Alexander, who later achieved brigadier
rank and whose brilliant memoirs[10] may be the single best pri-
mary source on the army; and Frank Huger, a smart young West
Pointer.

S. D. Lee left the battalion to go west soon after the battle
of Sharpsburg, where he sent the battery's survivors back into
action with remarks that Figg quoted and appropriated for his
title: "You are boys, but you have this day been where men only
dare to go!" In a fond postwar letter, Lee recalled his words only
slightly differently: "You boys have gone to-day where men would
scarcely dare to go."[11]

Lee's successor in battalion command, Porter Alexander, also
recalled the artillerists' battle performance warmly. He wrote
after the war to the last commander of Parker's Battery to extend
his compliments "to every one of the dear old comrades of the
days when we were young & all *meant business* together—Oh the
dear old Battalion!" "We can look back on our record," Alexander
wrote to Lieutenant J. Thompson Brown, "with pride & satisfaction. 'Old Mars Robert' trusted us just as fully as we trusted him,
& that is the proudest record that any Army ever had."[12]

Whittet & Shepperson issued a double-broadside announcing
the release of Figg's book in 1885: "Just Published, 263 pages,
handsomely printed and bound, with Heliotpye Portraits of Nine
Confederate Officers." The publisher offered the title for $1.25,
with free shipping for prepaid mail orders. The prospectus printed
quotes from six Richmond newspapers and magazines and three
testimonials from Confederates associated with the unit.

The one veteran of the battery itself who was quoted on the flier, Samuel Patteson Weisiger, wrote from his home in Augusta, Georgia, to describe the "genuine and exquisite pleasure" he found in reading Figg's narrative. "The revival of old memories has been tender and touching," Weisiger wrote, "and I have lived over the days from '62 to '65." Poor Sam Weisiger had fallen prey to the draconian worldview of Captain Parker late in the war, being sentenced "to carry a rail on his shoulder for four hours a day for 30 days" for the high crime of being overheard saying that Parker "was a rascal." In a gorgeously worded rejoinder, Assistant Secretary of War J. A. Campbell pointed out that a nineteen-year-old boy's passing comment hardly cancelled years of loyal service, and judiciously admonished the court to heed Ecclesiastes 7:21: "Take no heed unto all words that are spoken, lest thou hear thy servant curse thee."[13] The passage of two decades obviously had left Sam Weisiger cheerful and forgiving of his mistreatment.

The Whittet & Shepperson flier also quoted Captain F. M. Colston, a battalion ordnance staffer ("a charming narrative"); Colonel Del Kemper ("a charming little volume of reminiscences!"); the Richmond *Dispatch* ("a most acceptable contribution"); the Richmond *Whig* ("greatly superior . . . to the greater number of war volumes that have been issued"); and four other regional periodicals.[14]

Although no surviving evidence establishes the size of the print run, scarcity today suggests a printing of about 500 copies—perhaps 1000 at the most. Enough turn up today in the rare book market to make it clear that notably more exist than do books published in 100 copies, but the title surely is a scarce one. Whittet & Shepperson used three different cloth colors for binding: dark green, royal blue, and brown. Identical elaborate gilt stamping adorns the spine and front panel of all three versions. No hint of precedence can be attached to any of the bindings. Presentation copies by Captain Parker and other officers, which might be presumed to be early releases, vary between the colors. Whittet & Shepperson apparently just used whatever bolts of cloth that were handy in the warehouse, with no purpose in mind. The green cloth shows up most often, and blue the least.

Royal Figg briefly served after the war as a Methodist minister engaged in charity work, but converted to Catholicism and worked primarily as a printer. In 1870 he reported that occupation to the census query. He labored in the printing trade in New York City for a time, before returning to Richmond and Whittet & Shepperson. In 1889, Figg was living in Richmond's Merchant's Hotel, 1320 E. Main Street, and listed his trade as printer. Sometime soon thereafter he removed to Norfolk, where he died April 28, 1897, in St. Vincent's Hospital in Norfolk, where he had been "for several years a patient," at the relatively early age of about 55. He is buried there in St. Mary's Cemetery.[15]

The author died too early to enjoy the full impact that his book had on his quondam comrades in Parker's Battery. Near the turn of the century, and for a decade and more afterward, survivors assembled regularly for reunions, marked by food and camaraderie and silk commemorative ribbons. Their correspondence referred

steadily to the book that so skillfully hymned their youthful experiences as soldiers. The 1903 reunion, for one example, offered
"an Oyster Supper . . . given in honor of dead comrades and selves
who participated in 19 pitched battles. . . . NO SPEECHES, but
he who fails to tell a war incident when called upon, or sing a
song, will be turned over to the firing detachment."[16]

Military experiences inevitably prove more bearable in old-age
hindsight than in initial experience. A sturdy veteran of Parker's
Battery who served the entire war without absences declared, after
the retrospective of thirty years, that his first battle, in which the
unit played an important role in the triumph at Second Manassas,
"was the happiest day of my life." "Doc" Howard insisted that his
entire three years in camp and battle with his Confederate battery
mates made up "the best and happiest days of my life."[17] The early
origins of Figg's memoir, much of it written within a half-decade
after Appomattox, afford extra credence to the work, because of
its appearance before the dawning of that late-life rosy glow.

The last known survivor of the battery, William McKendree
Evans, outlived Figg by a third of a century, dying six weeks after
Hitler invaded Poland and inflicted World War II on the planet.
Willie Evans took advantage of his longevity to establish himself as
an authority on all things Confederate, using political leverage to
make sure his own record reflected a minor promotion, and admon-
ishing battlefield-park authorities about their perceived mistakes.[18]

The stellar merits of Royal Figg's book continued to draw
favorable attention long after the last veterans vanished, but the
book drew a far narrower audience than it deserved.[19] That low

profile was the result of a small printing and the early date of publication, before a recovering South had money to buy books or time to pay them adequate attention. *Where Men Only Dare to Go* does not appear even once in the indexes to the standard Confederate sets *Confederate Veteran* (1893–1932) and *Southern Historical Society Papers* (1876–1959). Between them, these two classic sources number 92 volumes and some 50,000 pages. Virtually any southern book about the war that appeared after the launching of *Confederate Veteran* earned notice in the magazine's pages; Figg was just too early.

The thorough Douglas Southall Freeman, in the bibliography of his famous history of the Army of Northern Virginia, called Figg's book a "history of . . . a famous command of boys." Several compendia of Civil War eyewitness sources skip the book entirely, and one waxes foolishly dismissive. E. Merton Coulter, in his thoughtful *Travels in the Confederate States*, describes Figg's work as having "considerable value as a commentary on the wartime South."[20]

In a book published last year, I included *Where Men Only Dare to Go* in a listing of my favorite and most important Confederate books.[21] The choice was easy for me because Figg so deftly opens a window on the experiences of artillerists at war. A rich blend of bravery, rascally behavior, and drollery makes the book an important source. Figg's literate presentation makes the trip through his pages easy and rewarding. How many enlisted men in the army might drop "orthographical feat" into a narrative (66)?

Where Men Only Dare to Go is a Confederate classic. No

reprint has ever been made, excepting the sleazy, but currently ubiquitous, glorified photocopying usually called "print on demand." The reappearance of Figg's book after so many years will give a whole new audience a chance to appreciate the eyewitness report of a bright, observant young soldier who fought through the famous battles in the eastern theater.

Robert K. Krick
Fredericksburg, Virginia
July 2007

NOTES

1. Brown's comments about Figg in a letter to the noted historian Frederic Bancroft, June 15, 1903, copy in the author's possession.

2. For thorough details on the formation of the battery, and everything else about it, see Robert K. Krick, *Parker's Virginia Battery, C.S.A.* (Berryville: Virginia Book Company, 1975). The 1975 first edition appeared in a limited run of 500 copies. Parker's experiences before he recruited his battery can be traced in contemporary articles in the Richmond *Dispatch* in these 1861 issues: May 4, 24, and 29; June 7 and 15; November 6. The same newspaper discussed Parker's activities in 1862 on January 1, 3, 6, 7, and 18; and February 21, 24, and 28.

3. Figg's official Compiled Service Record in M324, "Compiled Service Records of Confederate Soldiers Who Served in Organizations From the State of Virginia," roll 325, National Archives. The date of initial recruiting and the mustering details are from Lt. J. Thompson's Brown's diary, copy in the author's possession. Figg's age appears on the mustering-in document; the physical description on his 1865 parole from Point Lookout prison camp. *1860 Directory for the City of Richmond*, 96 (interior title, "Ferslew's Richmond Directory"). Despite the directory listing, Figg also appears in the report of what must be his mother's household (1860 Henrico County census, 836): Malinda Figg, age 51, born Virginia, with a reasonably solid personal estate of $1500. The census reports Royal's age as 18.

4. Figg's 60th Virginia service file in M324, Roll 1013, National Archives; Johnny Lee Scott, *60th Virginia Infantry* (Lynchburg: H. E. Howard, 1997), 97; Lee A. Wallace, Jr., *Richmond Volunteers* (Richmond: Westover, 1969), 257-60. Lee Wallace's excellent brief history of the company traces its unlucky assignments. Both the 59th and 60th regiments came out of the temporary, ill-formed Wise Legion, and their early records are intermixed.

5. Figg described his detail to Kemper in the book (24). The war diary kept by Lt. J. Thompson Brown reports with more precision that the detail was effec-

tive August 1, 1862. Two of the fourteen rolls actually covered a full quarter, rather than just two months, so they record Figg's uninterrupted presence from mustering in through February 28, 1865.

6. Most, but not all, of Figg's listings in the street directories and census enumerations cited elsewhere call him Royal.

7. The tentative use of "Washington" as a middle name appeared in Robert K. Krick, Gary W. Gallagher, and Nathaniel C. Hughes, *In Taller Cotton* (Wilmington, N.C.: Broadfoot, 2006), 30. Chris "Hollywood" Ferguson supplied me with the details about Figg's ancestors' names, based on genealogical search engines to which he subscribes.

8. Robert K. Krick, *Parker's Virginia Battery, C.S.A.*, rev. ed. (Wilmington, N.C.: Broadfoot, 1989).

9. Several impeccable sources confirm the composition-into-type story, these among them: J. Thompson Brown letter to Frederic Bancroft, June 25, 1903; my conversations in the early 1970s with Figg's two surviving nephews, Robert L. Figg, Sr., and Harry McGehee, of Richmond; an editorial in the Richmond *News Leader* in late 1939 (the clipping includes no precise date), which cites the diligent local historian Herbert T. Ezekiel. Ezekiel's good books, which establish his strong historical pedigree, are *The Jews of Richmond during the Civil War* (1915), *The History of the Jews of Richmond* (1917), and *The Recollections of a Virginia Newspaperman* (1920). Willie Evans of the battery told the tale to Daniel Grinnan, who wrote it on the flyleaf of a copy of Figg's book, owned by Stuart E. Brown, Jr., of Berryville (himself the grandson of a Parker's Battery gunner). The most interesting and conclusive evidence about the tradition came in a conversation that I had on June 3, 1974, with Mr. R. McLean Whittet (born 1890) at the offices of Whittet & Shepperson. Mr. Whittet had heard the story from his own youth with the firm, beginning not long after Figg's venture. He also produced a colleague who had heard the story, and received a copy of the book, from James Whittet, owner and manager of the firm in 1885. Unfortunately, although hardly surprising after all the years that have passed, Whittet & Shepperson had nothing extant in its files about Figg's employment there or on the size of the print run or any other publishing details.

10. E. Porter Alexander, *Fighting for the Confederacy: The Personal Recollections of General Edward Porter Alexander*, ed. Gary W. Gallagher (Chapel Hill: University of North Carolina Press, 1989).

11. Stephen D. Lee to J. Thompson Brown, June 29, 1906, copy in the author's possession. Figg's slightly different version is on page 44.

12. E. P. Alexander to J. Thompson Brown, July 1, 1906, copy in the author's possession.

13. Court martial recommendation signed by W. S. Barton, to A&IGO, December 23, 1864, and Campbell's rejoinder of the same date, in Weisiger's Compiled Service Record, M324, Roll 326, National Archives.

14. Kemper's full tribute, which includes some amusing self-deprecation, appeared in the Richmond *Dispatch*, June 25, 1885.

15. 1870 Henrico County census, 480; *Chataigne's Directory of Richmond, Va* . . . (1889), 235; Richmond *Dispatch*, April 27, 1897; Norfolk *Dispatch*, April 27 and 28, 1897; burial records from funeral director Harry Oliver, located for me by Mrs. Eleanore M. Hoover of Norfolk (her letter to me, June 10, 1975). The information on the record came from L. C. Figg of 2114 Venable Street, Richmond. The Rev. Fathers Doherty and Frioli—spelling uncertain in transcription—conducted the funeral service. Figg's brother, city police commissioner Lysander C. Figg, lived 1833–1910, according to relatives living in 1973. The Richmond obituary put Figg's age at 54, the Norfolk obituary says 56. In his stint as a charity Methodist minister, Figg ran the Seamen's Bethel Church, which stood across the street from the famed Libby Prison.

16. Broadside, Parker Battery Association, A.N.V. . . . May 24th, 1903.

17. T. C. Howard to "The Memorial Bazaar," April 26, 1893, Museum of the Confederacy.

18. An example of Evans's late-life declamations is his letter of April 22, 1935, to F. M. Chichester, of the Fredericksburg Battlefield Park Association, rejecting the standard contemporary accounts of the last meeting of Lee and Jackson. In a letter to Henry R. McIlwaine, September 21, 1928, Evans urged inclusion of his promotion to corporal in the rosters maintained at the Virginia State Library (where the letter is in the unit's file in the Adjutant General Papers, often called "the Bidgood Papers"); he did not mention his subsequent demotion back to private.

19. Freeman described the funeral of the battery's last survivor, with whom he often talked, in *Douglas Southall Freeman on Leadership* (Shippensburg, Pa.: White Mane, 1993), 131-32.

20. Douglas Southall Freeman, *Lee's Lieutenants*, 3 vols. (New York: Charles

Scribner's Sons, 1942-44), 3:821; Allan Nevins, James I. Robertson, Jr., and Bell Irvin Wiley, eds., *Civil War Books: A Critical Bibliography,* 2 vols. (Baton Rouge: Louisiana State University Press, 1967), 1:88; E. Merton Coulter, *Travels in the Confederate States: A Bibliography* (Norman: University of Oklahoma Press, 1948), 93. Freeman used Figg most extensively in describing the battery's first battle, Second Manassas.

21. Krick, Gallagher, and Hughes, *In Taller Cotton,* (Wilmington, N.C.: Broadfoot, 2006), 30.

PREFACE.

THE author of the following pages was, about two years ago, elected "historian" of the Parker Battery (veteran) Association. It was not contemplated then that he would do more than write a brief history of the company, intended only for its few surviving members and friends; but later he determined to write a book which would appeal to the general public for perusal—with what success the general public must judge.

The title of the book was suggested by the fact that the Parker Battery had a remarkable number of boys in it, many of whom were so young as to require the written permission of their parents to enlist, and by the speech (quoted from memory) of Colonel Lee, at Sharpsburg, when he said, "You are boys, but you have this day been where men only dare to go." The author was one of those boys, and he expresses opinions and sentiments with at least something of a boy's frankness.

During the three years of its service there were probably two hundred men who answered to the roll-call of this company; but many of their names will not be found here, as it was impracticable, in a work of this character, to give the personal history of each man. The names contained herein, however, are not fictitious, except " Robert Cannon," which was assumed by the writer because the narrative was necessarily personal.

Apology may be expected for the humble titles of the heroes of the story—only corporals, captains, and colonels; but the author endorses the sentiment of Delaware Kemper (who is only a " Major " in the book) that, "in these days, plain ' Mister' is a decidedly higher title than the military ones so complacently assumed by those who displayed their shrewdness, if at all, in keeping away from the scenes where real titles were won." Apology is certainly due to *General* Kemper for dismissing him into retirement with his wound at Manassas, whereas he served with distinction subsequently in the South.

Thanks are returned to Adjutant-General James McDonald; Rev. Dr. J, William Jones, of the Southern Historical Society; and Mr. Charles Poindexter, of the State Library, for courtesies extended the writer in the preparation of this book.

WHERE MEN ONLY DARE TO GO

THE STORY OF A BOY COMPANY.

CHAPTER I.

ORGANIZATION AND CAMP LIFE.

"'The design was that the wards should be, in their young years, taught the deeds of chivalry, and other virtuous and worthy sciences.'"—*Minor's Institutes*.

"MR. CHRISTIAN, would it be *right* for me to join the army?"

This question was asked by a young man of his pastor, in the spring of the year 1862, in the city of Richmond, Virginia.

"Certainly, Robert, it is right to fight for one's country," was the Rev. Mr. Christian's reply.

At this period civilian attire was extremely unpopular in Richmond, and even the "dim, religious light" of the sanctuaries of God afforded no friendly obscurity to those who did not wear the gray. The texts selected by the ministers and the tone of their discourses were of the most war-like type. Little was said about the Prince of Peace and the angel-song of good will to men; but "the LORD was a man of war," and He was implored to speak from the cannon's mouth.

Less than a year previous, the State of Virginia,

in sovereign convention assembled, had absolved her
citizens from allegiance to the United States of
America, and the emblem of secession, which Mar-
maduke Johnson had derisively described as "that
miserable caricature of the stars and stripes," became
the banner of *our* country, under which he, and
hosts that thought with him, marched to battle, and
many to wounds and death.

"Robert, I suppose you are a secessionist now?"
said a gentleman to me as I was passing through the
Capitol Square the morning after Virginia seceded.

"No, sir," was the prompt reply; "but *I am a
Virginian.*"

This was the epitome of a political creed.   Loyalty to the Union was treachery to Virginia; and
rude and shallow-minded must that Northern man
be who would call me a traitor.   No New England
boy ever loved the Union more than I, nor had the
right to love it better.   Why should my country's

> "rocks and rills,
> Her woods and templed hills,"

be less dear to me than to him?   Why should the
countrymen of Carroll and Marion and Washington
be less loyal to the true and the right than the countrymen of Franklin and Hancock and Warren?

My mother wept when the starry emblem of national unity was slowly lowered from its staff on the
Virginia capitol; and then she allowed her boy to
go and fight it!

"If this be treason, make the most of it"!

The spring of 1862 found the infant Southern Confederacy nerving herself to continue a contest the magnitude of which only then began to be appreciated by the masses. Roanoke Island had been taken by the enemy, and with it our brave Jennings Wise had surrendered his life. Fort Donelson had fallen, attended by an immense loss of southern territory and many men captured, with a ridiculously brief list of killed and wounded. In the midst of these and other disasters the term of enlistment of many of the troops expired, and the armies had to be reorganized and reinforced for the coming campaigns.

The martial enthusiasm of the Southern people was now at its height. The robbing of the cradle, if not of the grave, was begun early in the war. Beardless boys, as well as stalwart men, hastened to answer the call for more troops.

It is of a company of these boys that I wish to write, in order that some record of their manly deeds may be made before all recollection shall be lost in the haze of fast receding years.

On the night of the 14th of March, 1862, in the city of Richmond, Virginia, this company was formally mustered into the Confederate service, with Dr. WILLIAM W. PARKER as Captain. It was originally intended for the infantry service, our Captain having served the previous year as an officer in the Fifteenth Virginia infantry. Soon after we went to Camp Lee, however, it was decided to devote our martial energies to field artillery,—which fortuitous circumstance may perhaps account for the large number of survivors who are left to tell the tale of our toils and dangers. Infantry is notoriously the most "unhealthy" branch of the service, and its path to glory is too glaringly distinct as the path to the grave—at least for young patriots of a sensitive nature.*

At Camp Lee the boy company was drilled for several weeks. The experience was new and enjoyable. There was still an abundance of food and raiment in Richmond. "Hard tack," which a few years later was esteemed more precious than gold, was playfully arranged as paving-stones in front of some of our tents. In those days we did not deign to cook our rations, but negro slaves performed that and all menial duties for us.

We were formally religious—at least in Mess No. 1. Henry A. Atkinson, Jr., was "captain" of this little soldier family. My memory is not distinct as to Henry's rank in saintliness, but either he, or some one designated by him, regularly conducted morning and evening service. Profane or obscene language was discountenanced. There were also religious services which the whole company attended.

---

* The Virginia Life Guards, an infantry company, was organized in Dr. Parker's office in April, 1861. He entered it as a private. The first volley fired in the war was by this company, at Big Bethel. The Northern newspapers reported it as a "masked battery;" and the saying, "We proceeded cautiously among the masked batteries," had its origin here. The Life Guards were in a deep ditch in a graveyard.

We had no chaplain. At one of these prayer meetings, the "leader" (a private), seeing Captain Parker in the audience, asked—

"Captain Parker, will you lead us in prayer?"

"Yes; let us pray," curtly responded the Captain.

Why did he not kneel meekly, like one of us, and lead in prayer, without that " Yes; let us pray"? Are not all men equal—on their knees? Does not Saint Paul say "there is no difference"? But it seems that this man would be our Captain even when *in forma pauperis*. This was my thought *then*.

A memorable incident of this period was our attendance as a company, one pleasant Sunday morning, at Union Methodist church. At the conclusion of divine service, as we were marching out, the choir sang—

> " When shall we meet again,
>   Meet ne'er to sever ?
> When will Peace wreath her chain
>   Round us forever ? "

From Camp Lee the company was ordered to a point just east of Richmond. As yet we had not received field-pieces, but manned some heavy guns at battery No. 5, in the inner line of defences. A thunder-storm of appalling grandeur occurred about this time. The "bolts of heaven" seemed more than an equal rival to the far-flashing, "red artillery." This storm is associated in our minds with the battle of Seven Pines.

At a camp near Oakwood cemetery one of our

most beloved boys, William M. Evans, was painfully wounded by the accidental discharge of a pistol in the hands of William Parr. Evans recovered; and I only record the incident because, though an accident, it was the "first blood" drawn.

Soon after the battle of Seven Pines one of our men had an embarrassing experience as a sentinel. Posted at the intersection of several roads, he had orders to allow no one to pass except for good excuse. He must have construed his orders very liberally, or what follows could not have occurred.

"Halt! Who comes there?"

"Fourteenth Louisiana; going after rations."

There were several of these Louisianians, and the sentinel thought they might be just a few too numerous for the purpose in view; but "going after rations" was a pleasant phrase to soldier ears, and he let them pass.

This party was scarcely out of sight when the sentinel had occasion again to cry out—

"Halt! Who comes there?"

"Fourteenth Louisiana; going after rations," was the answer.

If it was right to let the others pass, it is right to pass these also, thought the sentinel; and so he allowed the second batch to pass. But when, after a while, a third crowd of soldiers answered the usual challenge by the reply, "Fourteenth Louisiana; going after rations," that sentinel thought the excuse was growing a trifle monotonous, and mildly requested them to return to camp, as it was scarcely necessary for a whole regiment to go on detail for one regiment's food !

The most pleasant camp-ground the company ever had during this period was on the farm of Mr. John Stewart, on the Brook road, about four miles from Richmond. Our tents were pitched among pleasant shade-trees not far from Mr. Stewart's residence, and the men had the advantage of the rustic seats and arbors in the beautiful grounds adjacent. Cherries, and perhaps other fruits, were abundant, and a request to eat of them was always answered by a pleasant "Help yourself" from the lips of the hospitable landlord. On Sundays we attended the pretty little Episcopal church (Emanuel) in the neighborhood, marching in military order to and from the sacred edifice.

From this secure and sequestered spot we heard the roar of the seven days' battle between Lee and McClellan. The reader need not sneer. It was a few weeks of rest for this boy company, preparatory to years of long and arduous marches. It was a little while to enjoy balmy sleep and abundant food, and then the midnight vigil and days of fasting. It was grass of unstained green and winds that whispered low and sweet, to be followed by the whiz of bullet and shriek of shell, and fields all reddened with human blood.

After the seven days' battles around Richmond the company was furnished with light artillery pieces and assigned to a battalion, with Major Delaware Kemper as commander—a brave and gentle man.

The writer, who, at Stony Run and for some time subsequently, was detailed as orderly for Major Kemper, has most pleasant recollections of his manners. Orderlies do not usually sit at the same table with field-officers, but Major Kemper made no such distinction, and presided at our camp-board with the same true politeness that one expects from a gentleman in civil life. Though a severe wound he received in our first battle deprived the country of his further service, his name is suggestive of all that is noble and kindly to those who were brought in contact with him, and to us of the boy company especially.

From Stony Run the company was ordered to Malvern Hill. There seemed to be indications of a fight, and we, to whom the "baptism of fire" was as yet a thing of anticipation, were much exercised over the prospect. We were getting "used to war's alarms" at least; and when, in a few days, we were ordered back to Richmond, and knew that we would soon be on the march to meet General Pope in northern Virginia, we began to feel like real soldiers. It was good-bye, sweetheart; good-bye, sister; good-bye, brother; but, more frequently, Good-bye, *mother!*

> "Stranger, tread lightly;
> 'Tis holy ground here."

If this can be written of heroes' graves, what pen is worthy to epitaph the sod where *mother* sleeps? He erred who wrote "there's nothing true but hea-

ven"; for mother-love is true. Yet mother-love is
of heaven,—

> " For Christ, who in the Virgin
> Our motherhood has blest,
> Is near to every woman
> With a baby on her breast."

O soldier-boy! be ye sure that mother's love and
mother's prayers will follow you on the weary
march, and be with you in the shock of battle; and
be patient with the weak in their hour of trouble,
and gentle to the fallen in your hour of victory,—
FOR HER SWEET SAKE!

CHAPTER II.

" The brave man is not he who feels no fear,
For that were stupid and irrational ;
But he whose noble soul its fear subdues,
And bravely dares the danger nature shrinks from."

Joanna Bailie.

"YOU are just where I wanted you; stay there."

This was the message sent by General R. E. Lee to Colonel S. D. Lee, our new battalion commander, in the early dawn of the 30th day of August, 1862.

The boy company had completed its first long march, and now stood on its first great battle-field. From the lowlands below Richmond we had pressed on until our eyes were gladdened by the blue hills that are laved by the waters of the now historic Rappahannock. Near Warrenton we had engaged in an "artillery duel" with a Federal battery, resulting in little damage to either party, but giving us some intimation of the experiences of war. Pressing on, with our faces still to the north, on the night of the 29th of August we passed through Thoroughfare Gap, on the way to Manassas Plains. It was about 2 A. M. of Saturday, the 30th, when we halted in some woods on the road-side. We had been marching almost incessantly for three days and nights. The boys dropped down, fatigued to exhaustion, glad to rest if but for an hour. As Billy Cogbill lay down, he noticed that the man next to him seemed to be sleeping soundly, although we had been in camp but a few minutes. Cogbill's suspicions were aroused. He shook the man, and found that he was dead. He wore the blue, and had been killed in these woods during the fighting on the previous day. Lieutenant Brown directed "Major," his servant, to wake up a supposed member of our battery asleep too near his horse. "Major" pulled the sleeper vigorously by the leg, which, to his utter consternation, gave way; whereupon he ran up to the Lieutentant, exclaiming, "I can't woke dat man, sah, dough I'se pulled his leg clean off, sah!"

At daybreak we were aroused by picket-firing on our right and left, and to our surprise found we had been sleeping within five hundred yards of the enemy. We were then ordered to fall back, and take position on a commanding eminence.

Thus the boy company found itself on its first great battle-field, in a line of eighteen guns, at a point just between Jackson and Longstreet. These were the batteries of Captains Parker, Rhett, Jordan, Eubank, and Taylor. Rhett's battery was commanded by Lieutenant William Elliott, and we had, in addition to our battalion of sixteen guns, a section of two "Parrotts" belonging to Grimes' battery, under Lieut. Oakum. These guns were placed in position about dawn by Colonel S. D. Lee, after consultation with General J. B. Hood; but before sunrise Colonel Lee had reported their location to General Lee, and he sent word, "You are just where I wanted you; stay there."

"Tell Uncle Robert not to forget my battalion to-morrow," was the message our commander had sent by a courier to General R. E. Lee the evening before the fight.

Here we had a grand view of the plains of Manassas. The sun had now risen in unclouded splendor. Before us the land broke beautifully into hill and dale, forming a sort of amphitheatre. The enemy had posted two strong batteries in our front. On their right and rear long lines of infantry could be seen, and far in the distance clouds of dust obscured the heavens.

As yet no solemn boom of artillery had broken the stillness of that pleasant summer morning. We have time to think. Strange and thrilling are our emotions. There were men doubtless on that battlefield who, sated with life or gifted with the peculiar military spirit, were almost eager to rush into its dangers. I saw an officer (not of our company) rise in his stirrups and shake his fist at the "Yankees," as he cursed them loudly and bitterly. Not many of us, however, as we look upward to the clear sky, and forward to the threatening enemy, are anxious to pass under the dark canopy of war.

Testaments are taken out and read quietly, and silent prayers are uttered.

"Cannoneers, to your posts!" was the thrilling command that now broke the solemn quiet.

The rifle-guns were ordered to "fire at the men in the corn-field." A few shots stopped their advance, and caused them to scatter and lie down. Then commenced a cannonading between our batteries and those of the enemy, which was kept up, with intermissions of fifteen or thirty minutes, during the entire morning.

It was now past noon, when a Federal regiment advanced rapidly to our right, determined to drive out our pickets, who were occupying a barn and an orchard. This effort succeeded, and our sharpshooters retired through the orchard in good order. So soon as they got well out of the way, we opened upon the enemy, and in ten minutes they "skedaddled" in fine style, sheltering themselves in ravines and behind the barn.

In the meanwhile the Federal forces that had been moving almost the whole day towards our left began to move in the opposite direction, and it was thought that they were retiring towards Manassas, about three miles distant. Several weak demonstrations were now made against our left, but a few shells served to scatter the skirmishers and drive them into the woods that skirted the valley on either hand. Almost every officer in our battalion was now of opinion that the enemy, foiled in his attempt to make us bring on the fight by these little advances, was about to retire, and merely kept up the cannonading to conceal that intention.

It was about 4 o'clock. Colonel Lee and Captain Parker were lunching together, when up rushed Private Barker, gesticulating wildly, and exclaiming, " Here they come, Captain ! Here they come !"

Heavy masses of the enemy, partially screened by the woods, were seen rapidly moving to our left, with the evident intention of breaking Jackson's line at the now famous railroad-cut, and taking our batteries by the flank.

In an instant Colonel Lee, always cool and self-possessed, ordered every howitzer to the threatened point, and as we galloped thither the enemy opened on us sharply.

"Go it, Parker, jumped over hell and gone!" exclaimed Davy Richardson. Just then a bullet struck him, and he was left to ruminate on the horrors of war while his comrades hurried on.

Lee planted artillery so thick at this point that cannoneers almost elbowed each other. On come the long, deep lines of the charging Federals, while at the same time their artillery opens furiously. No sound is heard but the roar of cannon and bursting of shells. Every man is at his post. No talking; no ducking of heads now. All is intense earnestness. It is an hour big with each man's history. The face is flushed; the eyes full; and the arm stronger than is wont. It is a struggle for life. It seems that the very heavens are ablaze; or that two clouds, surcharged with electricity and wafted by opposing winds, have met in terrific struggle. Just then I saw the recklessly brave Captain Taylor ride so near the muzzle of our rapidly firing howitzer that its blaze seemed almost to commingle with his horse's tail.

To our left the heroic infantry of Jackson are fighting with terrible earnestness. Their ammunition is exhausted, and they seize stones out of the earth and hurl them at the foe! When the enemy attempts to reinforce the lines that are pressing Jackson, Lee's batteries pour a withering enfilade fire into their ranks, and they waver and break.

See! by scores they are falling out of line, and then by hundreds and thousands. From a walk they hasten into a run, with the yell of our charging infantry sounding like the shriek of the storm-winds in their rear!

At this moment Silas Stubbs ran up to Captain Parker exclaiming—

"Captain, the Yankees are running! Let us give thanks!"

"Give them a few more shots first!" was that officer's characteristic reply.

Now the scene changes. Our infantry pour down from left and right upon the retreating foe, and our artillery ceases firing, lest we kill our own men; but the guns of the enemy blaze the faster, as if in desperation. On our right Longstreet closes upon them, and the hills roar with musketry. The sound of battle recedes, slowly but steadily, like a great storm of a summer's day.

It had lasted only half an hour!—that is, the roar and rush of this great charge. I awoke as if from a

terrible dream.   Yes, I am living, thank God!   Are
many of our boys killed?   Not one!   David Richardson and James Jones are wounded, but not mortally.   Our beloved Major Kemper is wounded, and
a few others in the battalion.   War is a gay thing,
after all, think we.   The "Yankees" will keep on
running, and if they dare to stop we can easily whip
them again.   But "Linden saw another sight," and
so shall we.   Sharpsburg loomed grim and ghostly
in the fateful future, but we saw it not; and Antietam was murmuring our death-song, but we heard
it not.

The gallant and effective service performed by
Colonel Lee's artillery in the second battle of Manassas has been the subject of eulogy from many
distinguished critics.   Thus General Lee himself
said that under its "well-directed fire the enemy's
lines were broken, and fell back in confusion."
President Davis said of Colonel Lee : "I have reason
to believe that at the last great conflict on the field
of Manassas he served to turn the tide of battle and
consummate the victory."

Colonel Heros von Borcke, of General Stuart's
staff, thus writes :

"The close columns of the Yankees emerged suddenly out of the dark green of the opposing forest
at a double-quick, five extended lines, of intervals of
sixty yards, comprising, at the least, fifteen thousand
men.   Their colors were borne proudly aloft, and
they advanced across the open space before us in
beautiful order.   Nearer and nearer they came, each

one of us looking on with hushed anxiety at the imposing columns which moved towards the Confederate position as a waterspout moves over the deep. The silence was something appalling, when, at the instant, forty pieces of artillery poured a withering shower of shells into the very midst of the advancing host, while at the same time their first line was received with a perfect sheet of fire from our triple infantry line concealed in the dense undergrowth of the forest. The artillery was in charge of Colonel Stephen D. Lee, and the accuracy with which the shells exploded in the very faces of the foe testified to the admirable service of the guns. It was as if an annihilating bolt out of the thunder-cloud had let loose its fury upon those doomed men, who until now had been pressing onward like moving walls, and they now wavered and swayed to and fro as if the very earth reeled beneath their feet. Again and again roared the thunder of our guns, again and again deadly volleys sent their hail of bullets into the dense ranks of the enemy, until all at once this splendidly organized body of troops broke in disorder and became a confused mass of fugitives. The Federal officers did their best to reanimate them. With the utmost energy and courage they brought their men forward to three successive assaults, and three times were they hurled back, leaving hundreds of their number dead and wounded on the plain. At last physical strength and moral endurance alike gave way before the terrible effect of our fire, and the whole force fled in disorderly rout

3

to the rear. At this moment the wild yell of the
Confederates drowned the noise of the guns. As
far as the eye could reach, the long lines of our
army, with their red battle-flags lit up by the evening sun to a color like blood, were breaking over the
plain in pursuit. It was a moment indeed of the
intensest excitement and enthusiasm. With great
difficulty could the cannoneers be kept back to their
pieces; and scarcely could we, the officers of the
general staff, resist the impulse to throw ourselves
with our victorious comrades upon the retreating
enemy."

After this eloquent roar of rhetoric from the
gallant Von Borcke, read the calm words of Captain Parker on the same subject: "Several writers,
Dr. Dabney among them, describe our artillery fire
as most destructive—making 'lanes' in the enemy's
columns. I went down and over all the ground traversed by the charging column, and could only find
132 left on the field—most of them dead, but not
more than a dozen killed by our 'terrible' fire.
I was so much impressed with the feebleness of the
enemy's 'charge' that I had the fence in our front
removed, and twice ordered 'Limber to the front,'
intending to gallop down on the right flank of the
column, and, at four hundred yards, give them 'canister,' but as I had no orders, and was quite a novice
in the artillery service, I countermanded the order.
From subsequent experience I am satisfied that such
a movement would have been eminently successful
upon the already demoralized enemy. The charging

column numbered about five thousand men. . . . . .
I visited all the battlefields about Richmond soon
after the fights there, but never saw such disparity
between our losses and the enemy's. I think I saw
five dead Yankees to one Confederate."

General S. D. Lee, now President of the Agricul-
tural and Mechanical College of Mississippi, thus
writes to the author, under date of November 7,
1884 : " Porter's entire corps did not amount to over
10,000 men. It was only the front lines that charged
across the field ; the reserves never got very far out
of the woods. I should say 5,000 Federals crossed
the field, about the same number in the reserves,
and were driven back by our artillery. It is likely
that the large number of Federals visible from our
ridge, who rose to meet Longstreet when he charged,
and also Jackson when he pursued, may have misled
Colonel Von Borcke. As you recollect, the fight
only commenced at 4 P. M. All who were on that
field witnessed, from that time till dark, a scene
granted to few : 90,000 American veterans, on both
sides, engaged in a death struggle, with the setting
sun calling time on them. . . . . I find Federal
writers say Porter had 7,000 to 12,000 men, and he
lost on that field (August 30th) about 2,200 men
killed and wounded. I think Captain Parker under-
estimates the losses on the field. My recollection is
that there were many more dead on the field than
he gives."

The reader now has before him the evidence as
to " who killed Cock Robin," and to what extent he

was killed. He has read the eloquent description of
Count Heros Von Borcke, whose name is a synonym
for martial prowess; the criticism of Major Parker,
one of the "coolest" men in the Army of Northern
Virginia; the later strictures of Lieutenant-General
S. D. Lee, who had every opportunity to see and
hear; and, prefacing all, the general remarks of a
short-sighted private, who saw very little but heard
a great deal. Gentle reader, you are thus left to
your own cogitations as to how we won the famous
victory of Manassas Plains.

The result of this battle was that the boastful
General Pope, who had entered the campaign with
his "headquarters in the saddle" and the expressed
determination to see only the backs of his enemies,
was compelled to retire upon the defences of Washington. The official estimate of his strength at the
beginning of the campaign was 74,578 men, while
that of General Lee was only 49,077. General Lee's
loss in killed and wounded was reported to be 7,241;
that of General Pope must have been much greater.

From the official report of this battle, which has
been kindly furnished me by General S. D. Lee, the
following extract is made: " Our position was an admirable one, and the guns were well served. Two
of my batteries were firing for the first time, but
did remarkably well. I cannot speak in too high
terms of officers and men under my command. All
behaved well, exhibiting coolness and courage. . . . .
I would mention the following officers as having
especially attracted my attention by their good con-

duct, viz.: Major Del. Kemper, who had his right
arm shattered by a minie ball; Lieutenant and Adjutant W. H. Kemper; Captains J. S. Taylor, Jordan, Parker, and Eubank; Lieutenant Elliott, commanding Rhett's battery; Lieutenants Taylor, Gil-
bert, Brown, Ficklen, and Oakum."

The evening shades are fast falling upon Manassas
Plains, where Federal and Confederate have or the
second time met in fierce and bloody combat. The
sounds of strife grow fainter and fainter in the distance, as the stars come out, one by one, and look
tenderly down upon the dead and dying. Here is
one—a mere boy. He is sleeping his last sleep.
On his bosom is an open letter, and the handwriting
betrays the gentle sex of the writer. Its sentiments
are beautifully pure as well as tender, and in it she
says: "I have not heard from you for a long, long
time; but I know that you will think of me, even if
you are dying." The leaves of a near-by tree rustle
softly. Is it the evening breeze? Or is it an angel
whispering of peace and love and life immortal?
"LOVE IS STRONGER THAN DEATH"!

CHAPTER III.

SHARPSBURG.

"Well do I recollect how that noble company of beardless boys performed the duties of veteran soldiers and patriots, second to none in the noble Army of Northern Virginia. Well do I recollect my thoughts on the bloody field of Sharpsburg, as I looked into the faces of the poor boys stretched in death around the guns they had so gallantly manned."--*Lieut. Gen. S. D. Lee.*

"ATTEND to those horses, sir, or I'll have you strapped to a caisson!"

The eyes of Colonel Lee flashed anger, and the tone was loud and haughty, as he spoke these words to one of "the men" of the Parker Battery, soon after the battle at Manassas, as we were going into camp near Leesburg.

It seems that a cannoneer had substituted for a driver on the march, and the driver was taken sick, thus leaving the cannoneer in charge of the horses. The cannoneer was one of that class of city boys who knew but little about horses, and was especially ignorant of the duties of a hostler, and was rather proud of that ignorance than otherwise. As soon, therefore, as we entered camp, this young-man-afraid-of-his-horses reported the situation to Captain Parker, who was seated at the root of a tree. He decided that the cannoneer, having had the benefit of the ride, and the regular driver being sick, must attend to the horses.

"Captain, I didn't enlist as a driver; I'm a cannoneer, and I don't know anything about horses," petulantly objected the man.

"Attend to those horses, sir, or I'll have you strapped to a caisson!"

This voice was as startling as thunder from a clear sky, as the cannoneer had not seen Colonel Lee, who was seated near Captain Parker, and had heard the whole colloquy.

"Hell hath no fury like a woman scorned,"—nor a man either, for that matter. The man, who felt himself to be "as good as anybody else," darted one look of hate in answer to the insulting words and angry glance of Lee, and walked slowly away. But not to the horses. Down into the woods he wandered, and the darker and deeper the shades the more congenial were they with his perturbed heart. Perhaps the only person whom that man ever really wanted to kill was Stephen D. Lee! It was hours, perhaps, before the evil spirit was exorcised, and he returned to camp. But not to those horses! And he never heard anything more of the matter.

Lee was the officer who was destined to win our soldier-love in the great battle soon to be fought at Sharpsburg. I say "soldier-love," for is it not true that men love a brave man—almost idolize him— in time of danger, simply because he is brave?

In a few days our boys were crossing the upper Potomac. The river was shallow and clear, and

some of us dallied merrily in its bright waters, glad
to be so refreshed after the tedious, dusty marches
of the past month.   Yet to how many was the fording of that river a type of the crossing of the mystic
stream

> " whose narrow tide
> The known and unknown worlds divide " !

Up the steep banks of the other shore we toiled,
and away through the fruitful fields of Maryland.
Then across the beautiful Monocacy, and into Frederick.   Never should we forget the kindness of at
least some people in that city to our needy boys,
especially that of the saintly ladies of the Catholic
Academy of the Visitation, the doors of which were
open to every soldier visitor.   These ladies filled
our canteens with molasses and gave us bread, but
did not forget to offer amulets and gently suggest
to us the mortal contingencies of battle.

The battle of Sharpsburg was to us the most sanguinary of the war.   Here, on the ever memorable
morning of Wednesday, the 17th of September, in
about two hours, at least a third of our men and
horses were killed or wounded.

On the evening previous to the grand conflict,
just as the opposing forces were nearing each other
in preparatory movements, occurred an incident
which is amusing in retrospect, though at the time
it was difficult to appreciate the humorous.   We
were under a heavy artillery fire, and bullets also
were too plentiful for comfort.   Twilight was deep-
ening into night, when a shot from a Federal battery

passed through two horses, casting quite a deluge of blood and flesh upon Private Clark, who was holding them.

"Lieutenant, my brains are out!" he feebly exclaimed.

"Then you have the biggest brains I ever saw!" replied Lieutenant Brown.

Little doubt was entertained at that moment, even by the Lieutenant himself, that these would be Clark's last words. You can scarcely imagine Clark's satisfaction, however, when the real source of the sanguinary baptism was discovered.

Blue jacket and gray lay close together that night, ready at the peep of dawn for the harvest of death. For these men were not the reapers; they were only the sheaves. Pride, Hate, and Oppression were the reapers, and as viewless spirits held high carnival that day.

That night the order was that the men must sleep by their guns, ready for action at a moment's notice. This order was a very broad intimation of what was expected in the morning; but we were still farther warned when, about midnight, we were startled from our slumbers by the report of a musket from a heavy piece of woods directly in our front, and then another report, and another, until it broke out into one continuous roar of musketry; and as I raised my head it looked as if the whole piece of woods was afire. Had we not been lying down, I think that some of us would have been killed then, as I heard the bullets whiz over me pretty lively.

That 17th of September was indeed a *dies iræ*—
a day of wrath. Lee's army stood on that bloody
day as one to three against the advancing hosts
of McClellan; and of all the enemy's generals Mc-
Clellan was the most feared. Our men had been
subsisting mainly on green corn and fruit since our
advent into Maryland, and many of them were sick
and weak; but when the "long-roll" calls to battle,
or the bugle sounds the advance, the true soldier
must not think of hunger or weakness. Thus Lee's
thirty-five thousand men stood defiant before Mc-
Clellan's one hundred thousand in that harvest-field
of death.

The fight commenced at break of day, and by sunrise the smoke of battle hung like a pall over the
scene of conflict. Men and horses fall in rapid succession. "Kenny" Richardson (a boy of fourteen)
and Corporal Newell are killed; Trueman falls
mortally wounded, and Lieutenant Parkinson, and
Cook, Tumbridge, Duffey, and Bolton are more
or less severely stricken. Parker and Brown are
the only commissioned officers left to face this storm
of bullet and shell, but they are gallantly sustained
by the Cogbills, Hallowell, Ned Moore, and Saville.
The charge in one of the guns explodes prematurely
and sends its "rammer" whizzing over to the enemy, at the same time burning and almost blinding
dauntless George Jones, who even then will not
leave his post.

A shot crashes through a caisson, and McNeil,
who escapes as if by a miracle, significantly holds

up the blessed beads given him by the good ladies at Frederick.*

"Darden," says Captain Parker to "the coolest man on the field," "Darden, if I am killed, tell my wife I was never happier in my life"! †

When it seems as if nothing can live under this withering fire, Colonel Lee orders the gun of Sergeant Hallowell to be advanced! Obedience is the watchword of this thrilling moment, and forward we move to go still deeper into the tempest of death! Not only in front, but from the flank the enemy pour their fire into us. A shot ploughs through the bowels of our lead horses, and crushes the leg of Warburton, the driver. The two remaining horses plunge wildly about, trying to extricate themselves from the fallen horses in front. At this critical

---

* If any one is inclined to smile at McNeil for holding up his beads at the moment he so strangely escaped from death, let me tell him that I carried one of these "charms" in every battle that Parker fought. I have one now, a relic of the historic past, which was given me, in 1863, by Miss Julia Winston, of Caroline county. It is made of paper and printers' ink, and is called the Holy Bible. A word is but "the sign of an idea." If paper and ink may symbol faith and hope, why may not beads? And if any one sneers at both blessed beads and blessed book, let me tell him that scoffers were scarce where bombs and bullets were flying thickest. I know that there are bold bad men as well as brave devils ; but if the fate of my country had to be decided by a selected few, I would prefer to risk my all with the Stonewall Jacksons and—the McNeils.

† Major Parker desires the author to say that the "happiness' spoken of was of a religious character, and not that he would like to die fighting.

moment Joe Hay, with his pocket-knife, cuts the harness, and we are then ordered to fall back.

We do not go far, however, when, under the lead of the brave Captain Taylor, of the battalion staff, Sergeant Hallowell's gun attempts to take another position; but we are only wheeling for the purpose when an artillery shot explodes over us that kills Bryant, our remaining driver, and mortally wounds Captain Taylor. As Taylor falls from his horse, Darden and I catch him in our arms, and his hero-blood spurts all down my jacket sleeve, and dyes the gray into its own sanguinary hue. Intrepid George Goff springs into the saddle made vacant by the fallen Bryant, and we withdraw from the field.

We are now allowed to rest awhile, after which Colonel Lee made us a short speech, which still rings in my ears. I can recall, perhaps, his very words, although more than twenty years have elapsed since that fateful day, for they are written in letters of fire on the tablet of memory. He said:

"You are boys, but you have this day been where men only dare to go! Some of your company have been killed; many have been wounded. But recollect that it is a soldier's fate to die! Now, every man of you who is willing to return to the field, step two paces to the front!"

As Lee spoke these words he seemed a very god of war, and his eyes flashed command, not entreaty.

Weak and almost dazed by the scenes of horror through which we had passed, stern Duty calls, and we obey. The significant "two paces" is stepped, and a volunteer section, led by Lieutenant J. Thompson Brown, returns once more to confront the now exultant enemy.

On the way we pass a pond of water—yellow and hot and stagnant beneath the blazing September sun. Raging with thirst, I stoop and drink; some others do the same. Weak, sick, thirsty, hungry,— forward we go!

The gallant sergeant Harry Jones, of the brave old Fayette Artillery of Richmond, saw this volunteer section as it was going in, and, hailing it, was answered by the word "Parker's."

Through the town of Sharpsburg we pass, now crashing under the shot and shell of the enemy,— its streets covered with debris and wounded, with crouching women and children in its cellars,—until we reach a battery on the right of the road. This battery is briskly engaging a foemen who seems most worthy of its steel. Colonel Lee here leaves us, but before doing so orders Lieut. Brown to take position on a hill about a thousand yards distant. This hill is already occupied by two batteries that seem to be fighting at great disadvantage. Arriving at the foot of the hill, we find these two batteries in the act of leaving. As we pass them their commander asks,

"Who are you, and where are you going with those two guns?"

"To take the hill you are leaving," replies our gallant Lieutenant.

"I can't hold it with two batteries: how can you with two guns? Return with me, or you will be cut to pieces."

"I am obeying the orders of Colonel Stephen D. Lee," answers Brown. "Are you his superior?"

"No."

"Then, forward men!" And we are where we were ordered to go.

"Did Colonel Lee mean for me to go to the aid of those two batteries that were here when he gave me orders, but now nearly back in our lines? Or did he intend my two guns to buffet the storm two batteries could not stand?" thought Brown.

"Sergeant, report to Colonel Lee on yonder hill, and ask for further orders."

Our experience that afternoon illustrates how, when men have determined to do a difficult thing, the path seems strangely smoothed, and help comes when least expected. For some reason, the enemy do not reply to our fire briskly. Perhaps our noble infantry have too badly crippled him. We are so weak that when our gun recoils, we lack the strength to push it back into position. But the mere boys are still high in indomitable spirit as the sturdiest men. Little Sam Weisiger is there, and Willie Evans, the youngest of all, and the cheeriest and pluckiest of all.

The autumn sun is fast declining to his rest, as we continue to fire slowly and feebly. The enemy replies as if he, too, is weak and shattered. Sons of the North and sons of the South are lying thick upon the hillsides and in the valleys. Sharpsburg is groaning, and Antietam is running red; and there will be weeping among the blue hills of Virginia and on the banks of the Savannah, and the prairies will hear the voice of lamentation, and the Hudson will answer in bitter and melancholy refrain.

The sun is set, and bloody Sharpsburg is a thing of history.

Said the London *Times* of this battle: "Such dreadful carnage as that which has just taken place in America is unknown in modern times."

Said the New York *Tribune:* "One can imagine how furious the cannonade must have been from the fact that but five dwellings, in a village containing fifteen hundred inhabitants, escaped uninjured. The women and children were huddled together for three days in the cellars. One cellar, under a large stone mansion, contained more than sixty."

In a letter, written on the 18th, to the same paper, it is said: "We have been burying our dead and carrying off the battlefield our wounded. I have just returned from the sickening spectacle. Soldiers who went through all the battles of the Peninsula say Fair Oaks and Malvern Hill were as nothing compared with it. The dead do lie in heaps; the wounded are coming in by thousands. Around and in a large barn, about half a mile from where General Hooker engaged the enemy's left, I counted one thousand two hundred and fifty wounded. Along the same road, and within the distance of two miles, are three more hospitals, each having from six hundred to seven hundred in them, and long trains of ambulances standing in the road waiting to discharge their bloody loads. Surgeons, with hands, arms, and garments covered with blood, are busy amputating limbs, extracting balls, and bandaging wounds of every nature and in every part of the body. Rebel soldiers in great numbers lie among our own and receive the same attention. I saw a rebel officer, of the Twenty-seventh Alabama regiment, endure the amputation of his leg without the use of chloroform. Every muscle in his face was contracted, his jaws looked as if in a death-spasm, but no sound of pain issued from him. The saw and the knife did their work, but they could not wring from him an expression of physical agony."

Here let me pause to cast a flower on the grave of one of the sleepers on the banks of the Antietam. The noble son of a noble sire, John Crafton went forth at the command of Virginia, and stood bravely for her honor even unto death. Peace to his patriotic soul!

As Sharpsburg was a battle in which the boy company won so many bloody laurels, the reader is asked to pardon the presentation of another account of it as given in the letter below. It was written by

Captain Parker, and is copied from the Richmond *Dispatch* of September 30, 1862:

CAMP NEAR MARTINSBURG,

September 24, 1862.

As it seems many contradictory opinions prevail in regard to the fight at Sharpsburg, on the 17th instant, I think it may not prove altogether uninteresting to some of your readers to have a statement of facts which, though not complete, you may rely upon so far as they go.

On Sunday, the 14th, the corps of Longstreet was encamped near Hagerstown, between that place and a village called Funkstown. The artillery of General Pendleton and the battalion to which I am attached (commanded by Colonel S. D. Lee) encamped on Saturday, the 13th, near the latter village, and remained there till Sunday afternoon at 4 o'clock. Up to this time the army (I mean the body of it) was evidently under the impression that we would soon go into Pennsylvania. Why we did not go on faster was a matter of frequent inquiry; but such was the confidence in our Generals that no distrust existed, and no sort of anxiety on the subject. The army had preserved the greatest caution in Maryland in regard to private property, much more so than in Virginia, and this, too, to its great discomfort and inconvenience, and many wished to go on in order to get rid of this embarrassment.

When, therefore, the order came, Sabbath afternoon, to countermarch towards Frederick City, there

4

were many sad faces, and many earnest inquiries as
to the cause of this retrograde movement. The
people of the town saw us pass through their streets
with the same indifference that they beheld us enter
the town the day before.

We continued our march (the whole of Longstreet's corps) towards the " Gap," some eight miles
south, and when in three or four miles of it we were
halted, and I was informed, upon what I regarded
as the very best authority (a Brigadier-General), that
an artillery fight of no importance was going on in
the Gap, and that we had better go into camp.
From this encampment we could distinctly see the
shells of the enemy burst in the Gap where our men
were posted. This Gap is in the range of mountains
that separate Frederick City from Hagerstown. I
learned later in the day that the affair in this Gap
was more serious than at first supposed, and it was
said there had been mismanagement somewhere. It
seems but a small force had been left to guard it,
and that the defence had been committed to a subor-
dinate (a Colonel, I was told) who knew nothing of
the ground, and that General McClellan having
massed his large force there our men were badly cut
up, and but for Longstreet's arrival would have been
terribly handled. I was also informed that the army
would fall back towards the Potomac that night;
that Generals Jackson and McLaws were engaged in
an attack upon Harper's Ferry, and General Lee did
not think it prudent to engage the whole Yankee
force in their absence. This was the first intimation

I had of Jackson's absence, and I think this fact was not known to the army generally. It was thought that he was about Frederick City.

Our horses were kept harnessed, and at 3 o'clock Monday morning we moved by a private road towards the Potomac. At daybreak we encountered Longstreet's corps coming into the main road that leads to Sharpsburg and the ford at Shepherdstown, and the artillery and infantry moved on together. At about 11 o'clock A. M. we halted at a village called (I think) Garysville, and took position on some hills south of the town; but in an hour thereafter we moved on to Sharpsburg, a few miles further, and were posted on the hills south of this village.

This village lies in a deep valley. On the east is a high mountain ridge, running nearly from north to south, and all about the town are very high, bald hills. You do not often see a more broken country. Our centre, commanded (I think) by D. H. Hill, rested on the village; our right, under Longstreet, at the base of the mountain; and our left, under Jackson, about a mile to the left of the village—the spectator facing the east.

About 2 P. M., Monday, clouds of dust indicated the approach of the enemy, and before night some of his artillery had gotten into position, and several of the rifle sections of our battalion interchanged shots with him, but without much effect. Night came on and all was quiet, and we lay down by our pieces expecting that to-morrow the great struggle would begin; but the sun arose in all his glory, and still no sound of war was heard.

The country about Sharpsburg is exceedingly beautiful; the farm-houses and farms in the best condition.

As the day wore on many thought there would be no fight. The enemy was moving his forces to the right, and we once supposed he would make the attack there, and drive out our pickets at the base of the mountain, and attempt to turn our flank. At 4 o'clock, while Generals Longstreet, D. H. Hill, and Hood were observing the enemy from a point on the left of the town, near where our battalion was in position, large bodies of artillery and infantry were seen passing to our left through some low-ground just in front of us and beyond a stream which divided the two armies. With our glasses we saw them very distinctly. We were surprised at the number of ambulances that accompanied these troops. It was about 5 o'clock before the whole force passed through this meadow. As the train was often halted, I could not think it possible that the enemy would make an attack that evening, especially as it would take him some time to get into position. Others were of a different opinion.

Just to our left and front was a pine thicket, about five hundred yards distant, and the rear of the column of the enemy had hardly gotten behind it before very sharp picket-firing began. We had previously placed sharpshooters in this thicket, and so soon as the firing began others were put into it at a double-quick.

It was now nearly dark, but the picket-firing increased greatly, so that two howitzers were ordered from our battalion to hurry forward and support our pickets by shelling the woods. In the meantime the enemy's battery of eight guns, at which we had fired on Monday and part of to-day, opened upon our right flank, and the guns being twenty-pounder Parrotts, splendidly managed, did some execution in the darkness, though two thousand yards distant. In Parker's battery two horses were killed and one man wounded. The minie balls from the woods whizzed above us, but no other damage was done. The picket-firing was maintained till 9 o'clock, and indeed so often renewed during the night that it was difficult to sleep. It was now evident that the morrow would be a day of blood.

As we lay down upon the field, and look up into the great sky, we can but blush for the wickedness of man. Oh, how calmly and reproachfully do the bright stars move on in their courses! It was a beautiful night, and no man who lay upon that field, and realized the deep tragedy which was to be enacted on the morrow, could but be sad and thoughtful. The past was present as well as the future, and we scanned the three together and tried to learn wisdom from the study. We thought of dear ones far away, and were glad that they knew not of the trying hour that the setting stars were bringing rapidly on.

At 3 A. M. every man was at his post, and
awaited in solemn silence the day dawn.   No
sooner did the light break in the east than the
picket-firing began, and increased in fury until
about sunrise, when artillery and infantry together
grapple in the terrible fight.   Heavy columns of
Yankee infantry appear to our left and front in a
thin skirt of woods, and our guns pour into them a
deadly fire of shot and shell.   Our infantry on the
left were in line of battle under cover of a small
ridge and a corn-field, while sharpshooters were also
in the corn-field itself, between our line of battle
and the enemy.   We also had artillery just in front
of the thin woods through which the enemy advanced, and, as the distance was not more than four
hundred yards, it must have done great execution.
In about an hour, or perhaps less, the enemy brought
up artillery in the thin skirt of woods also, and
opened upon the guns in their front so sharply that
they had to be withdrawn.

It was then that they turned upon us both artillery and infantry, and the conflict was terrible.   The
eight-gun battery, mentioned before, far on our
right and free from attack from us—indeed, out of
range—opened with great effect, enfilading both
our batteries and the whole line of infantry.   They
got the range with the first shot, and kept it for
two hours.   But for this cross-fire the fight would
not have lasted two hours.   McClellan, it seems, had
compelled us to fight him where he could rake our
whole line, and had thrown such a heavy force just

at that point that it could not well be resisted; so
that, after four hours' fighting, we fell back about
six or eight hundred yards. On the extreme left,
however, we drove him more than a mile, and had
possession of his dead the next day.

At 9 o'clock the battery to which I was attached,
having twenty-one men killed and wounded, and
having also lost twelve horses, was ordered out of
the fight by Colonel Lee, and fears were entertained
that some of our guns might not be brought off;
hence we were ordered to throw off all baggage,
thus leaving some thirty of the men without blankets and overcoats.

The batteries engaged in this part of the field
were Captains Jordan's, Rhett's, Woolfolk's, Moody's,
and Parker's. Of some three hundred men engaged,
about eighty casualties occurred.

In the afternoon of Wednesday the enemy made
a very bold charge on the right, where Longstreet
commanded. They flanked our forces and compelled
them to fall back into a corn-field. Beautifully did
the dark blue lines come up the hill, and I greatly
feared the result when I saw their superior numbers
(four to one), but no sooner had they risen to the
crest of the hill than a most murderous fire was
opened upon them from the corn-field. With my
glasses I could see the gaps made in the line distinctly. On they came, however. Up came the
stars and stripes, waving in the wind; but some two
flags (all that I saw) went down; but up they come
again, and then, as if the flag-bearers were upon the

ground frightened or wounded, they are at "half-mast," and there remain until the whole line, now terribly thinned, gives back, and the colors disappear. Our boys now rush from the corn-field and pursue them down the hill.

This, I think, was the last severe fighting of the day. From morning till night there was cannonading, but I think the two affairs I have mentioned comprise most of the serious fighting done on Wednesday. I was, however, absent from the field for several hours during the day, having been ordered to the rear to refit.

On Thursday we expected the enemy would renew the fight, and we were ready to give him a warm reception. On the previous day we had not our whole force on the ground;—General A. P. Hill did not come until late in the day, and his men, and Jackson's also, were fatigued. But Thursday passed away, we holding some of the enemy's ground and he some of ours, and no disposition was shown by the Yankees to renew the contest.

But for the raking fire of the enemy's artillery, I am satisfied we would have whipped him in two hours. Our artillery ammunition is almost worthless. The shells and spherical case generally do not explode at all. Another disadvantage we labored under was the nature of the ground. It was almost impossible to charge batteries posted upon such high hills.

Under these circumstances General Lee (very wisely, I think) determined to recross the Potomac, three miles distant, and thus save the army from any possible disaster, and at the same time give his men rest and food, both of which they greatly needed. We recrossed the river Thursday night in the best possible order, not leaving behind a single piece of artillery. General Lee stood at the ford at Shepherdstown and gave directions to the teamsters and others, showing a wise attention to details which many men in less elevated positions would think beneath their notice.

As to the question who won the fight at Sharpsburg, I think it cannot be said that any decision was arrived at. It was a "draw fight," but, according to the Yankee confessions of loss, they certainly got the worst of it.

Before I close this letter, permit me to call attention to the noble bearing of Captain John L. Taylor (C. S. N.), of Norfolk, who, not wishing to be idle, asked for duty, and was assigned, some three weeks ago, to Colonel S. D. Lee's staff. This gallant gentleman I have seen in several fights, and he seemed generally to seek the hottest places. Colonel Lee, who seems himself fearless as one needs be, several times cautioned Captain Taylor about exposing himself, but to no purpose. On Wednesday, as we were leaving the field, and while I stood near him, he was shot in the neck, and fell speechless from his horse. He was put upon a caisson and brought off the field. He lived five or six hours, but was never sensible. Thus died as brave a man as any I ever saw upon any battlefield. He really seemed not to know what danger was. A daguerreotype of a sweet babe, which I took from his pocket, spoke to my heart in words more touching than poetry. God bless that babe and its mother !—the wife and child of a brave man and a patriot !

CHAPTER IV.

"WHO TAKES THIS?"

"The devil publishes his doin's—murders, and filthiness, and thievin'—ay, an' of hypocrisy and self-righteousness. But God keeps His grace growin' quietly, like the blessed corn or the spreadin' cedar. If ye want to prove it, ye must get some planted in your own heart. If you want to believe that other people do good deeds, do one yourself. When you've given a shilling in secret, you'll feel quite certain there's plenty more has done the same."--*Peter Smith.*

SHENANDOAH! legendary "daughter of the stars"! Pleasant are our memories of thee! Weary and battle-scarred, our battalions rest in thy sweet valley. What waters so pure and sparkling as burst in glad abundance from under the gray old rocks that buttress thy heaven-seeking hills? What grass so green as carpets the banks where thy quiet waters flow? What trees so beautiful and strong as tower in lordly grandeur even on thy mountain-tops, and toss their arms in proud defiance when "storm howls to storm and wind wars with wind"? But when the eye, sated with thy nearer beauties, looks out to where

> "The sunlight lies, like a yellow crown,
> Upon the beautiful mountains far away,"

but enclosing thee on every side, how instinctively

we think of the Holy City and its guardian hills, and its awful Sentinel who never sleeps! Well may we be reminded of the prophet's vision of celestial warriors—"the chariots of Israel and the horsemen thereof"—flaming in grand parade and guarding with eternal vigilance the land that even God called beautiful, and even He could love! In thy quiet shades His "still, small voice" is heard—

> " still on the evening breeze
> As once of old, the Lord God's voice
> Is heard among the trees."

Let us listen to it, and perhaps we may believe that at Sharpsburg were present not only men and devils, but good men and good angels, and that He who "worketh all things according to the counsels of His own will," finally will evolve out of Lust and Hate and Death, Purity more pure than the laughing waters, Love more infinite than the blessed sunlight, and life more lasting than the everlasting hills.

"Father, the rebels are not all devils, for one of them gave me a drink of water on the battlefield."

Thus spoke a wounded Connecticut boy, in a field-hospital near Sharpsburg, to his father, a Methodist minister, who had hastily come from his New England home to attend his now dying son.

"Yes, father, when our troops were beaten back, and I lay wounded on the field, one of the rebels stooped over me, and I feared he wanted to kill me, but he only said softly, 'Poor boy!' and gave me a drink of water."

It is said that

> " The bravest are the tenderest,
> The loving are the daring ";

but it may have been difficult for that Northern man, albeit a minister of God, to believe that the "rebels were not all devils," when he saw his dear son stricken and dying in the yet dewy spring-time of life, and knew that the fatal blow was given by a Southern hand. It is hard to forgive when the heart is first bleeding with a sense of great injury. Yet that dear boy died forgiving his enemies, and peacefully trusting in God. This incident I had from the lips of his brother, years since the cruel war; and the story was told me with such gentleness and tenderness that I found it in my heart to drop a tear with him to the memory of the sleeper at Antietam, though he wore the blue and I the gray.

Yes, "God keeps His grace growin' quietly, like the blessed corn or the spreadin' cedar." Sigh softly, O ye winds, over the graves of the gentle brave, and, ye snows, wrap them kindly in heaven's purest ermine, until that day when "the mystery of God shall be wound up."

We come now to a period in the history of the boy company when it ceases to be so boyish. An arduous campaign, including two great battles, has hardened them almost into veterans. Besides this, a number of them are disgusted and disheartened by our experience at Sharpsburg, and avail themselves of the legal plea of minority to leave a service that includes too much of hardship and danger to please those who had fondly hoped for fun and adventure. It may be candidly confessed, too, that some who remained did so more from considerations of honor and compelling circumstances than from enthusiastic devotion to a cause which, even the most obtuse could now see, must triumph, if at all, at the expense of many lives lost and homes desolated.

Camp living became less elaborate. Servants were conveniences of the past, except among the officers; and the camp-board began to evidence, if not a scarcity of food, certainly a most monotonous lack of variety. We drew fresh beef from the commissary so continuously that it sickened me to hear the report of the guns which told that more bullocks were being slaughtered. One morning I strayed near Captain's tent, and the smell and sizzle of the bacon that "Captain's Joe" was frying caused me to appreciate as never before the temptation of Esau; for I felt almost willing to barter the whole Confederacy, my birthright of liberty included, for a few morsels of that same fried bacon. Indeed, I did unbend most benignly, if not humbly; for the moment social inequalities and difference of color were forgotten, and Joe and I became brethren at the frying-pan of King Hog. Perhaps we were symbolizing the march of coming events; and perhaps, if all the "colored brethren" were as good as Joe Mayo, I would say to events, "March on!"

Six or eight men are standing around a camp-fire. Breakfast has been cooked, and is laid in six or eight separate little "piles" on a board near by. A man is standing near the board, and in front of him, with his back to the board, is another man. The man near the board is Andrew Barker, sometimes called "Yankee" Barker, on account of his supposed shrewdness, and he with his back to the board is James Darden, a man of the nicest sense of justice. It is the duty of Barker to see that each "pile" is as nearly equal as possible to the others, and then, putting his hand on one of them, ask "Who takes this?" to which question Darden, without looking, must reply by calling the name of any member of the mess, including his own and Barker's.

Everything is ready, and the "drawing" begins.

"Who takes this?" says Barker.

"Todd," answers Darden, and Tom Todd steps up and contentedly removes his "pile."

"Who takes this?"

"Hightower." And John Hightower claims his own.

"Who takes this?" again says Barker.

"Barker," answers Darden.

"No, you don't, Darden," quickly exclaims Barker, "No, you don't, Darden! It's the smallest pile on the board!"

It must be remembered that Barker had apportioned these rations, and he supposes Darden to have slyly peeped over the shoulder and called the name "Barker" for the "smallest pile."

"Who takes this?" got to be a by-word in the company, and "old mother Barker" got the name of being the sharpest and most provident as well as one of the bravest of our number.

Somebody composed some verses about this time that harmonized with the music of the bugle-call to feed horses. They run thus:

"Oh, get up, you drivers, and go to the stables,
    And water your horses and give 'em some corn ;
For if you don't do it, the Colonel will know it,
    And then he'll punish you as sure as you're born."

Some wag, more witty than reverential, parodied some well-known verses of Scripture somewhat after this fashion: "Man that is born of a woman, and enlisteth in Jackson's army, is of few days and short rations. He cometh forth at reveille, is present also at retreat, and retireth apparently at taps. When, lo! he striketh a bee-line for the nearest hen-roost, from which he taketh sundry chickens, and stealthily returneth to his camp. He then maketh a savory dish, wherewith he feasteth himself and a chosen friend. But the Captain sleepeth, and knoweth not that his men are feasting."

The night we fell back from Sharpsburg, in crossing the Potomac, we were allowed to ride on the caissons, while the infantry had to wade the river.

On the Virginia side was a detail of infantry for the purpose of shoving up wagons and artillery in case they stuck in the mud. As we approached them we were received with a shower of mud and stones, they saying it was bad enough to have to shove up the artillery without including "the d——d lazy artillerymen!"

One of our caissons broke down that night in the middle of the river. Charlie Murray was left to guard it until it could be gotten out. He said he stayed there until nearly morning, and, having a large piece of bacon he had "captured" in Sharpsburg, he was eating lustily, when up rode Stonewall Jackson, who remarked, "Well, sir, you seem to be enjoying yourself!" Murray politely asked the General to "have some," which invitation he quickly accepted. After eating a few morsels, Jackson told Murray that he had better move on, as the enemy was not far off, and rapidly advancing.

A vision rises before me. It is the face of Tom Kirtley—stern, almost solemn, with an occasional play of a grim sort of humor about the lips. He it was who said at Fredericksburg, at a time when we were all "hugging" the ground, "I don't want nothin' under me, not even a sheet of paper; but if there be paper, I don't want no writin' on it." Tom was of strong physical build, but clumsy, and his whole conformation indicated the slow sort of animal he was. Tough, too, he was; on bitterly cold nights, when officers shivered even in their buffalo robes, he would wrap himself in his thin blanket and sleep comfortably near the ashes of a smouldering camp-fire. At times he gave vent to ideas that indicated deep thinking, but so queerly that even his theological opinions would excite rather to laughter than to prayer. I first won his heart by being able to spell the name of his native village—McGaheysville, in the Valley of Virginia—an orthographical feat which he considered unparalleled. He trusted me, and many a night did we talk together, quietly and slowly, about the deep things in theology. Not that Tom used that learned word; but problems that have been unsolved by the deepest thinkers were stirring his heavy brain, and he was groping his way in the dubious domains of unexplored truth—sternly, doggedly. It seemed of little use to tell him that nobody knew anything about the origin of evil, and other mysterious problems; he was determined to invade the shadowy realms of the unknowable, and make his own peculiar deductions. Tom had a taste for the poetic, too; but, as you may anticipate, it was queer poetry that Tom liked. He unbosomed himself to me on this point under peculiar circumstances. It was under the frowning heights of Gettysburg, when we were in line of battle, and everybody knew that a terrible engagement was imminent.

"Do you know, Bob," asked he, "what I think is the prettiest poetry I ever heard?"

"No," said I; "let's have it."

"Well," slowly replied Tom, "it's this:

'The men of high condition,
    That rule affairs of state;
    Their purpose is ambition,
    Their practice only hate.'"

I replied that I thought his selection singularly appropriate to the occasion, but thought that I could beat it with something more hopeful, at least; and I quoted from a hymn I had learned in Sunday-school:

"The sword and spear, of needless worth,
    Shall prune the tree and plough the earth;
    And Peace shall smile from shore to shore,
    And nations learn to war no more."

"Say that again, Bob; say it again!" exclaimed Tom. "It's the prettiest thing I ever heard!" And his eyes gleamed with eager interest. Not until I had repeated this prophecy of the "good time a-coming" several times was he satisfied. He tried to memorize the words, again and again insisting that it was "the prettiest poetry" he ever heard. And you, reader, might have thought so too, if, like us, you were just under the shadow of gloomy Cemetery Ridge.

Poor Tom is in his grave now, but all the surviving Parker boys will keep his memory green as long as steady courage and a kindly heart shall be respected by them.

It was at Gettysburg, also, during a lull in the firing, that one of the boys in our company came up to me and "professed conversion." I was not a

chaplain—in fact our battalion of nearly a thousand
men never had a chaplain; but I was prominent
among the praying boys, and hence was often made
a sort of confidential adviser in things spiritual.
These battlefield "conversions" were not infrequent.
The one I allude to was quite emphatic and exhube-
rant, but not lasting in its results.   It certainly produced a marked change in the demeanor of its subject for several weeks, and until we were pleasantly
encamped somewhat remote from the enemy; but
not longer.   Laugh as we may, after the war, about
the noisy artillery, and how little it was feared, compared with the cold gleam of the infantry bayonet
and the deadly whiz of the minie; but I confess that
to my ear there was something mournfully suggestive
in the booming of cannon and shrieking of shell.
The minie may hit, and the object of its wrath may
live to tell the tale; but when the "solid shot" or
bursting shell finds its victim, it generally leaves him
a disordered mass of quivering flesh.   I repeat it,
there is something awfully solemn in the shriek of a
coming shell.   "Hark, from the tombs, a doleful
sound!"—"Awake, my soul, stretch every nerve!"
—"My thoughts on dreadful subjects roll, damna-
tion and the dead!"—with a liberal mixture of
"I'm a-coming, old Black Joe!"—seem, to the nervous ear, to commingle in one horribly solemn med-
ley, and no wonder that people got "converted" on
the battlefield.   I can tell how one of the popular
churches got a "D. D." within its folds in this way.
It is true he was a student, with at least one eye on

the ministry, when the war broke out; but the incident I am about to narrate certainly hastened his
entrance into the sacred calling.

Boanerges was one of those sanguine and sanguinary young men who predicted, several weeks
before the great struggle began, that "we would
manure Virginia soil with Yankee carcases." In
this humor of mind he bid farewell to academic halls,
and hastened to the "tented field." His company
soon found itself on one of the first battlefields of
the war, and there was a chance for the "manuring"
process to begin. But what if the cowardly Yankees
should object? The mountain region in which this
battle is pending is bare and sterile, and a few thous-
and Yankee carcases would help vegetation amazingly.
But see! they do object, the impudent fellows! Instead of coming forward in droves, like peaceable
sheep ready for slaughter, behold! from yonder woods
they are advancing in orderly line of battle, with
bayonets gleaming and flags defiantly floating. They
do not dare to fire any guns as yet, but their whole
demeanor is alarmingly belligerent. So thinks our
young Boanerges. The situation calls for prayer.
Our boys had thrown up some temporary earthworks, and behind them Boanerges kneels, and
prays with great energy, if not faith, "O Lord,
drive them back! O Lord, drive them back!"
Anxious for a speedy answer to this urgent plea, he
partly rises and asks, "Boys, are they coming or
going?" "Coming!" was the alarming reply. He
again falls to prayer, and, if possible, with more en-

ergy than before, implores the "Lord" to "drive
them back!" To his tremulous question, however,
"Are they coming or going?" the awful answer
still is, "Coming!" At last, after a third and most
urgent storming of the "throne of grace," Boanerges
is told that "the Yankees are going!" With this
news his martial energies are aroused. He seems a
very son of Mars as he springs upon the breastworks, defiantly exclaiming, "Come back here, you
cowards! Come back here! We'll whip you!"

The enemy had been only demonstrating, and
there was little or no fighting; but this experience
convinced Boanerges, and others too, that his talents
lay in another direction. He sought and obtained a
chaplaincy.

There were men who were made infidels by the
defeat of the Confederacy. They were men of
great faith as long as their "God" was doing what
they wanted Him to do. "Great faith"? Superlative impudence! Tremendous presumption! That
is, if this "God" was any bigger than his devotees.
Then was the time—standing amidst the ruins of
blasted hopes and shattered ideals—to learn something REAL about GOD!—in the valley of humiliation—at the foot of the Cross!

It is said that a lady, walking over the battlefield
of First Manassas, while yet the dead and wounded
were scattered here and there, exclaimed, "Oh, the
poor, fat horses!" Her heart was first touched by
the sight of the dead and dying brutes rather than

of the nobler animal, man. While I do not admire the preference of her sympathy or her manner of expressing it, the sufferings of our horses was for me often the subject of solemn thought. Everybody knows how grandly that animal figures in history, from Job's typical war-horse, whose neck is "clothed with thunder," down to General Lee's brave and faithful "Traveller." In battle how sympathetic with the occasion! When he first hears the roar of the conflict, he trembles, as men do, and his eyes gleam with startled interest. Perhaps he feels like retreating, and perhaps his master does too. The roar increases; the lightnings of battle are flashing around him, and its thunders crashing far and near. Does he tremble now? No! Like his rider, he has caught the awful inspiration of glorious war! To his ear the roar of conflict is now the grandest music; to his fierce eye the leaping flame from hostile cannon is beautiful! Forward he springs, and nimbly, bearing his brave rider to glory or to—— fiddlesticks!

"Yours truly,"—but not "very." "What is writ is writ," but the reader may take my war-horse *cum grano salis;* and give the horse some too. I expect he needs it. Salt, you know, is good for horses. If he isn't tired, his rider is. I got tired of him just about the time of that "leaping flames" and "glory and ———" incident.

Just here I am tempted to tell a little joke on the cavalry. Since the war I had an intimate friend who served in that branch of the service, which has

been tersely called the "eyes of an army." One
night, when the wind was howling around the house-
corners, grimly suggestive of ghosts and goblins
riding on broom-sticks, Hughes and I were seated in
our room by a cheerful grate-fire. We were so congenial that talk was unnecessary to make us company for each other. I fell to musing. Visions of
a cavalry fight rose before my mental eye. I had
never seen one, and the picture my imagination now
drew of charging troopers, swooping down upon a
waiting foe who is equally brave, and the sickening
slash of sabres into human bones and flesh that must
inevitably follow, made me feel weak and cold, although I was snugly resting in an arm-chair by the
fire. So I drew closer to "Hughsy," and unbur-
dened myself of the picture of bloody horrors my
imagination had drawn.

"Nothing of the sort, Bob; nothing of the sort,"
replied plain, practical "Hughsy." "The real fact
is, when we charge, we draw our sabres, put spurs
to our horses, and yell like Comanches; but when
we get close up, somebody's got to run! If the
Yanks don't, we do"!

It is of the common war-horse that I started to
write—especially he that dragged our artillery on
the long marches. Up the steep hills, down into
the deep mud of the valleys, only to climb another
hill. Pull! pull! Drivers cursing and whipping
him. On! on! until wearied nature breaks down,
and he falls in the harness. But this is not all. He

may be lazy, they think, and they whip him again, if perhaps the sting of the lash may arouse him to further exertion. Then, finding at last that he is of no further use, they leave him on the road-side to die. These men that drive him have volunteered to brave all the hardships and terrors of war; but, O God! what about this soulless horse? Soul-less? Ah, that's the question! "The creature was made subject to vanity, not willingly," says Saint Paul, "but by reason of Him that made it subject—in HOPE."

One chilly November day, in 1862, we receive orders to march. We must leave our pleasant camp near Winchester, and hasten over the mountains to the eastward, where General Burnside, the new commander of the Army of the Potomac, needs our attention. We are now fording the Shenandoah. The beautiful river is shallow, but its current flows strong and cold. The hardy infantry are wading through it by thousands, but we of the artillery, when we come to the water's edge, are allowed to mount our caisson- and limber-chests. Thus happily exempted from a semi-immersion in the chilling waters, we are conveyed to the other shore.

The clear, martial notes of Eglin's bugle sounds the advance, and we are now climbing the great, blue mountains. It was a romantic scene. The winding road, the long line of infantry and artillery, and Eglin's bugle ever and anon breaking the monotony of our tramping feet with its wild, ringing music. Toiling upward, we reach the crest of the great Blue Ridge, from whence far, far east, is seen wave after wave of gradually declining hills, calm and awful, like a petrified sea.

"Oh, Sergeant, how grand is this scene!" said I to Sergeant Hallowell. "It is worth all the toils and dangers through which we have passed!"

"Yes," replied he, "but some of us must pay a dear price."

Now, I remember his brave, honest face as a picture only of the past. He, the best gunner in Parker's Battery, and one of the best in the First corps, gave his life at Gettysburg for his dear Virginia, and the dew-drops of her blue hills and the tears of a bereaved wife commingle on his grave.

CHAPTER V.

FREDERICKSBURG.

"It was a gallant company, and no one will go farther than myself to give it praise."—*Lieut.-Gen. S. D. Lee.*

ON the 6th of November, 1862, Colonel Lee was commissioned a Brigadier-General, and assigned to duty in the far South. Before the close of the war he attained the exalted rank of Lieutenant-General. A soldier by education, he impressed men and officers alike as a strict disciplinarian. The writer, whom he once threatened to "strap to a caisson," has a lively recollection of his disciplinary abilities. It is not thought that he ever strapt a soldier to a caisson; but he did tie them up sometimes, which was about as bad. His strictness, however, was commended by its impartiality. He made no distinction against the private soldier, nor in favor of the commissioned officer. In fact, my recollection is that he was more popular among "the men" than among the officers. I have seen him send them in disgrace to their tents for bungling in drill. Of course in this retirement they prayed for their beloved superior.

We of the boy company were used to strict discipline. Our martinet Captain did not spare the rod in his military family; and if Colonel Lee never "strapt a soldier to a caisson," Parker did. After saying this about the strictness of our Captain and Colonel, the reader will pardon me for expressing the opinion that if all the officers in the Confederate armies had been, even in matters of discipline, like Lee and Parker, the cause for which they fought might not necessarily be epitaphed as "lost."

November, 1862, found the battalion encamped near Culpeper Courthouse. Two guns of Parker's Battery occupied an advanced position, where there were some indications of a fight. It was about dark one cloudy evening when we received orders to "limber up" and march. Quietly, almost stealthily, we press on through the dark woods and under a starless sky. We know not where we are going, nor is it our right to know. The wintry clouds threaten rain, and the winds moan ominously through the dark forests. "Forward, march!" is the substance of our knowledge and duty.

It was probably about noon of the next day, under a still threatening sky, that we reached the Rapidan river. "Raccoon" is the name of the ford. As usual, the cannoneers mount the caissons at the margin of the stream. When we are about the middle of the river, an officer rides up and inquires,

"Why are you men on those caissons?"

"Colonel Lee always lets us ride at the fords," promptly replied big-mouthed Sam Weisiger.

"Colonel Lee does not command this battalion! Get down at once!"

Weisiger and the other boys still hesitated to jump into the chilly river, saying, "Do you really, order us, sir?" The man on horseback assured us of his sincerity by drawing his sword, at sight of which gleaming emblem of military authority we all quickly submitted to a semi-immersion in the middle of the Rapidan. O could our mothers have seen us then!

The officer with the drawn sword is E. P. Alexander, of Georgia, the successor of Lee as our battalion commander, and destined, like him, to higher rank. He is not a tyrant, but the uplifted sword is the emblem of lawful authority that must and shall be respected.

Rain! rain! rain! How it poured for days, and made the red Culpeper mud almost as slippery as ice! Tramp! tramp! tramp! Artillery, infantry, and horse, night and day! Burnside is threatening Fredericksburg, and mud and water is made a test of Southern patriotism in lieu of a warmer element. How many a "d—n the Confederacy!" was uttered on that march, even by those who wore the "stars and bars"! The chilly November winds, and dark, weeping skies were not propitious for patriotism of the fiery type. The "boys in gray," who, a year or two previous, expected to have a pleasant time "playing soldier," on that march obtained a farther insight into the hardships of war.

The muddy road is so slippery that we can hardly retain our foothold, and Darden and I jump the

fence and walk in the field parallel with it. It is
night, and still raining. Darden is the man whom
Parker pronounced the "coolest" man on the fiery
field of Sharpsburg. He is cool now—very. Po-
litically he is an original secessionist; ancestrally,
the son of a Methodist minister, and worthy of his
raising; physically, he is very tired and wet; and
mentally, he is thinking ———, what the Dutchman
paddled Hans about. As yet he has not expressed
himself, but there is a storm within that rivals the
one without. On we trudge in the rain and darkness. Presently we come to a ditch, or what seems
to be one. It is so dark that we cannot tell how
wide it is, or deep. I jump, and clear it. Darden
jumps, and flounders in the ditch, and I help him
out. Patience at last ceases to be a virtue, thinks
Darden, and he expresses himself freely and recklessly. He cannot curse; but the way he "dog-
goned" Jeff Davis and the Confederacy would have
been popular talk in a "Yankee" camp. So thinks
the silent comrade trudging on by his side, and a
mental note is made for future reference.

Late in the night we stop in some woods for rest.
It is with great difficulty that a fire is started, as rain
still pours. At last we succeed in making a blaze;
wood is plentiful, and we are soon warming ourselves
around a cheerful fire. "Polly, put the kettle on."
But there is no Polly, and so "old mother" Barker
and his assistants have to make their own "tea." In
fact, it was a sort of beef tea, or thin soup, with an
abundance of red pepper in it, that we made that

night. This soup was very hot, and produced a perspiration. Very unhealthy, any physician would say; especially as it still rained, and we soon lay down and slept in our wet clothes and blankets. Yet nobody was sick next morning; but Ransome, a tall, fair-complexioned young man, died soon thereafter,—perhaps from exposure.

Near Fredericksburg, on the night of the 10th of December, 1862, Colonel Alexander came to Captain Parker and said: "General Lee has information that the enemy will attack us, on the right, just before day. The signal for the attack will be a solitary cannon-shot. So soon as you hear this, take your battery to the line of battle."

True to this warning, while it was yet dark, on the morning of Thursday, the 11th, the boom of the signal gun broke the stillness of the night, calling our sleeping army to march and to battle. The long-roll drum-beat of the infantry, and the shrill blast of the bugle, commingled in martial confusion, while statedly the sound of the signal gun, reverberating through the pine woods, seemed to say, "Prepare! Advance!"

It was a clear, frosty morning, as, with our horses at a gallop and cannoneers mounted, we took position in the line of battle. Fredericksburg and Marye's Hill is to our right. In front is an undulating country, with here and there a grove of trees and a farmhouse; then a canal; then the Rappahannock river, and beyond all the Stafford Heights, crowned with

Federal artillery of heavy calibre. These heights
are soon obscured by smoke from the guns. Under
cover of this fire the Federals are crossing the river
on pontoons. They are stubbornly met by General
Barksdale and his Mississippians; but the artillery
fire from the Stafford Heights is very severe and
the Federals press across the bridge in vastly superior numbers, and our infantry fall back—slowly,
stubbornly.

While an active fight was kept up far to our right,
we were occupied during the day with the artillery
posted on the other side of the river, and only had
one man painfully wounded. About a thousand
yards to our front was a canal, and fearing the enemy
might cross it at night and assault us, our Captain
suggested to Colonel Alexander to let him take one
gun and go to the Stansbury house, some five hundred
yards in front of our main line, where General Mahone had some infantry in ambush, so that if the
enemy should attack us at night the artillery would
be close at hand to help. After dark the gun was
taken down and concealed behind the Stansbury
house, while the horses were put into the basement.
The order was that no man should show himself.
Picked men were stationed behind trees, and commanded to keep a sharp look out. One of these
men was short-sighted, but the occasion was not propitious to make known this infirmity to our Doctor-
Captain. So he said to David Brown, his comrade:
"Davy, you tell me when the Yankees are far off;
I'll tell you when they come close."

The morning of the 13th December, the decisive day of the battle, while the guns of the battalion crowned the hills in our rear, this gun, under the immediate eye of Parker, was thus masked behind the Stansbury house. The enemy must have suspected our whereabouts, for they begun to fire at the house from their heavy batteries on the Stafford Heights. As shot after shot tore through the massive brick mansion, smashing window-glass and precipitating bricks upon us and the horses, it was very difficult to maintain self-composure, or for the drivers to hold their horses. In the meanwhile the grand charge against Cobb's brigade, at the foot of Marye's Hill, was in progress. From our position we could distinctly see the charging lines of the enemy; how bravely they moved up, like billows of the sea, against the grim stone wall; then recoil in disorder; the officers rallying the men; and again and again the plucky Irishmen return to the charge. The roar of musketry and deep-toned bellow of cannon is awful to hear. We are doing nothing— but trying to maintain our own composure and obey the order, "Don't show yourselves." I recollect about this time, just as a solid shot came thundering through the house, that I lost, for a moment, self-control, and called out, "What's the order? What's the order?" As these words escaped my lips I recollected that my duty was simply to obey the order already given, "Don't show yourselves." But nowhere during the war do I recollect being the subject of such ungovernable excitement, as when, behind the Stansbury house, and within sight and sound of the great conflict at Marye's Hill, my duty was—to do nothing.

Moreover, from our position we could see the arrival of train after train from Washington filled with Federal troops. I thought they would never cease coming. Oh, how the heart ached lest our boys should be worn out by these repeated assaults from fresh troops!

It occurred to Captain Parker that something must be done to stop the rallying of the enemy under the cover of a little ridge in front of the stone wall. Not being able to get orders from Col. Alexander, he requested General Mahone, who spent most of the day at the Stansbury house watching the fight, to permit him to go over to Marye's Hill and get the Washington Artillery to train a gun on this rallying ground. The ride was a hazardous one. His route for a mile was through an open field, swept by the fire of a Federal 12-gun battery. It had been a desert all day which neither man nor beast had trodden. But reaching his destination in safety, he got an officer to train one of his guns on this rallying ground, which at once changed the face of matters in that locality. It was found by the enemy a bad place to stop or stay, and, when repulsed by Cobb's men, they continued their retreat beyond this point. Had this gun been thus directed sooner many a brave Irishman's life would have been spared. In this attempt to save the Irishmen's lives our Captain came near losing his own. He failed to notice that all the men in this battery went half bent, in most (w)holesome fear of a large number of sharpshooters just in their front; but they gave him no warning. Wishing to get a good view of the fight at that point, he rode carelessly up to an embrasure in the breastworks, and, raising himself in the stirrups, essayed to take a calm look at the scene below. Judge of his horror, as he cast his eyes down under the hill, to see a dozen or more men, their guns at rest in loop-holes in an old brick tannery, taking dead aim at him, and the next instant the sound as of a flock of small birds filled the air. They were unfeathered messengers of death. Throwing his body forward on his horse's neck, and burying both spurs into his flanks, he fled from the horrid spectacle.

It was now about 4 o'clock, and hearing from some infantry in rear of the battery, that only twenty thousand of our men had yet been engaged, he could but exclaim with exultation, "The day is ours!"

On returning across the same ugly field to the Stansbury house he observed that the Washington Artillery was still doing excellent service in preventing the reformation of the repulsed enemy in front of the stone wall.

Now that the day was won, we longed to see the sun go down; but it seemed that some Joshua had commanded it to stand still.

Willie Evans, a boy of sixteen, was detailed as courier for Colonel Alexander during this fight.

He was sent with orders to Captain Grandy, who
held a position to the left of the Plank road leading
out of Fredericksburg, and nearly in front of the
tannery at the foot of Marye's Hill. This building
was filled with Federal sharpshooters—the same who
gave our Captain such a lively salute. Grandy's
guns were in breastworks, and it was "unhealthy"
for a man to show any part of himself. Alexander's
orders to Captain Grandy were that he must open
fire as soon as he heard the signal gun from Jackson.
The question with Evans was, how to get to him.
Suddenly his horse stops, and trembles under him,
as if preternaturally warned of danger ahead. It
seems like certain death to ride up in fair view of
the marksmen concealed in the tannery; but he must
deliver the orders to Grandy. An odd plan occurs
to him: he will dismount, and roll down the hill!
No sooner thought than done. He got off his horse,
and she had sense enough to lie down in a fence-
corner, and down our courier rolled right into the
breastworks! What Grandy and his men thought
of this mode of delivering dispatches he did not stop
to inquire. Returning he found his horse waiting
in the fence-corner, and they soon showed their
heels to the "Yanks," to their mutual comfort.

The reader may begin to think that my warriors
do too much running, and I am willing to concede
that their courage is most happily tempered with
discretion. It is a sentiment most ignominious, but
still it is written, that "a live dog is better than a
dead lion." Not that this canine-leonine metaphor

can be justly applied to my boy-heroes; but most everybody, you know, in the moment of mortal peril, felt like he would be willing to endure a few more weeks of the hardships of camp life—for the sake of his dear country. Besides, in winter-quarters we could go to see the ladies in the neigh-borhood, and they evidently preferred a pleasant chat with a live soldier to "a good cry" over the "dear departed." Fredericksburg, too, is a battle in which we are not destined to die very numerously. The casualties in the boy company may be stated thus: Killed, 0; wounded, 1. If the reader com-plains of this bloodless literary diet, he must seek some other caterer; for I protest that I will not kill any considerable number of our boys, even with printers' ink, simply to gratify his appetite for the horrible. But fearing that he may think us too discreet, let me point him to yonder horsemen, rid-ing along the line of battle, where shells and bullets are bursting and whizzing. They are Colonel Alex-ander; our German bugler, Eglin; and Willie Evans, courier. Alexander stops, and gives the reins of his horse to Eglin. He has just seen a flock of par-tridges, who seem to have lost their little senses in the infernal uproar. Poor, dazed things, they flutter about, not knowing whither to fly. Alexander cooly draws his pistol, and opens fire on them—for amuse-ment! "Dunder and blitzen! Mine Gott in himmel!" exclaims Eglin (aside) to Evans, "What make the Colonel such a tam fool!"

But we must return to the Stansbury house. By

the aid of General Mahone's engineering skill, our
Captain found a spot from which we could enfilade
the enemy in front of and beyond the stone wall,
and we worked all night to get the gun in position;
but it turned out that the enemy did not renew the
attack, and the work was useless.

As soon as it was dark, Captain Parker hurried
over to our guns on the right, near Fredericksburg,
and was anxious for some officer to go with him to
General Lee and urge that one hundred guns be
turned upon the town, now crowded with the worn-
out enemy. He was satisfied that we had almost
the whole Federal army under our guns, with little
hope of successful resistance. He felt the impulse
to make the attack was *instinct*, and therefore cor-
rect. But getting no encouragement to go to General Lee, he determined, without orders, to fire into
the town with his own battery. In directing the
fire he was aided by the church steeples. There
were many lights in the town, but our firing soon
extinguished the last one of them. I think we fired
all the ammunition we had. The enemy made no
reply.

The day after the battle was Sunday. Andrew
Barker and I walk down the line to Marye's Hill, and
from that point view the scene in front of the stone
wall. The morning is cold and damp. The town
of Fredericksburg and the Stafford Heights, with
the river winding between, are seen at a glance; but
nearer, in the low ground in front of the stone fence,
is a spectacle that fascinates the eye with a sickening

tenacity. The bodies of hundreds of brave Irishmen lay cold and nude in the winter sunlight, some with their arms outstretched towards the fatal hill, as if indicating their last brave thought. Among these heroic remains are moving creatures in human shape who are stripping the dead whom others have not stripped. O ye guns on Stafford Heights, why are ye silent? O ye quiet Sabbath heavens, slumbers no thunderbolt in your holy depths that ye will let loose upon these ghouls in human shape? "Andrew, I am sick—sick; let's go away." And I lean —and need to lean—on Andrew Barker's friendly arm as we slowly turn our backs upon the heroic dead of Meagher's Brigade.

Ah me! the church-bells are calling to prayer from many of Columbia's hills, and the cross still rises as a holy symbol in Killarney's vale; but, O God! where is man's love for man? *

Soon after the battle we went into camp a short distance to the rear. It was a snug pine-thicket where our tents were pitched. No one but a soldier can fully appreciate what a protection these thickets were against the bleak winds of winter. Hardened by exposure, and with the warm blood of youth and health coursing through our veins, a fire is scarcely necessary to us, even in wintry weather, if only the cold winds are broken by a friendly hill or cosy pine-woods.

---

* A friend suggests that "a lack of clothing to protect a living body from wintry cold is excuse enough for robbing the dead." Be that as it may, I give my own impressions.

It was in one of the thickest and cosiest of these thickets that we went into camp after the battle of the 13th December, 1862. Our mess is lucky to have a real cook among its members, and Marion Francisco, the fat little Corsican, can make soup and pastry that would tempt an epicure. "Old mother" Barker has been careful to obtain a beef-shin from the commissary, and we are all sitting around a blazing wood-fire, on which is boiling a huge camp-kettle of soup. Each man has a tin cup and spoon, and presently, seated on logs, we are all eating supper. What delicious soup it is! What tender boiled beef, and delightful corn bread! Spiro Zetelle doubtless might make soup as good as did our Corsican caterer, but his larder could not furnish the sauce—a Confederate appetite. You will not find this sauce in any of the jars or bottles in any of the stores or saloons. You want the recipe? Well, I'll tell it you, but on condition that you will not report me to the druggists and doctors; for its use will injure their business. Just these three things: Sunlight, Fresh Air, and Exercise. Mix well and use moderately; and if you are not too old, or prematurely aged from unnatural living, this sauce will produce a Confederate appetite; and that means joyous health—that is, if you don't have to depend upon a Confederate commissary! But in the winter of 1862 we had a plenty of substantial food and some luxuries. Around this camp-fire we eat and talk, and talk and eat; but for a while there is decidedly more eating than talking. At last—with even a Confederate hunger satisfied—pipes are produced, and the dreamy wreaths from "Killikinick" and "Zephyr Puff" rise slowly in the odorous air. There sits Darden, whom Weisiger has pronounced "as brave as Agamemnon and as cold as an iceberg." He looks too comfortable to remind one of ice-bergs, but we all know that under his cold, passionless exterior the fire of a strong nature burns, yet a fire under control of a master will. Near him is George Saville, whom we have lately elected lieutenant, but who has not yet left us to consort with those of his own rank. There is also soft-mannered Phil. Scherer, quiet, kind-hearted Tom Todd, pious but hot-tempered Silas Stubbs, and (as I wish to save some compliments for the next chapter) a number of other fellows; and just over at another fire is a whole family named Roach, for Roaches we did have, and a number of them in our soldier family; and at this camp-supper was an Orange and a Figg, with three members of the Royall family—young Tom, "old hairy" Tom," and Willie Royall, of the "far-flashing red" Richmond Howitzers.

Presently there is a stir in the pine-thicket just behind us, and out stalks our "noblest Roman." Of medium height, a perceptible stoop as he walks, but active as a cat; strong grey eyes, and a moustache that is the opposite of meek in its luxuriant growth, our visitor stands before us in the flickering fire-light. We rise and respectfully salute him; for this man needs no "commission" from Government to enforce his claim to be the real Captain of "the boy battery," and Parker's quick, sharp "Good evening, boys," is answered by several eager invitations to "Take this seat, Captain." Of course the softest side of a "soft-pine" log was not too good for the Captain; and even if there happened to be a gnarled limb against which he rested his notorious "backbone," who cared for the expense?

He will not smoke, but he can talk, and the smaller guns are silent.

"Well, boys, the night before the battle, as you know, was cold and damp. I could not sleep in the open field we occupied, and, there being not a stump or log on which I could rest my body, I had to walk about to keep warm. If I can get a stump or log to sit on, I can sleep very well, leaning on my hands. Many a night have I slept well in a drenching rain, with my head through a hole in my oil-cloth, and not get a drop of water on me. But that cold night I looked in vain for a place of rest. Seeing Tom Kirtley coiled up in a thin blanket near a handful of smouldering coals, I thought, as I had a bear-skin lined with thick bocking, I might get a nap too; but in fifteen minutes the cold from the snow underneath so chilled me that I was compelled to get up. Tom Kirtley, who seems to be a sort of cast-iron man, was sleeping soundly. I had not gotten far from Kirtley before I thought I heard the low wail of an infant. I listened intently. An infant out on this cold night, at two o'clock, in this bleak field! Impossible! But the sound is now more distinct. It seems to approach me. Peering through the dark, misty night, I see the shadowy outline of a tall figure. Is it an apparition? It moved noiselessly towards me, its size, doubtless, magnified by my imagination. I said, 'Who comes there?' 'I am a woman flying from Fredericksburg, where I have been hid with my baby in a cellar,' was the response, in a womanly voice. She was stately and calm, and hugged her infant to her bosom. She said she did not know which way to go, and begged that I would direct her to the nearest house. After giving the desired information, I resumed my cheerless beat; but a fire was burning in my heart, and I thought, Would God I could hasten the sun-rising that I may defend innocent women and children!'"

As we listened to the Captain's narrative, we all felt that it would be rather unhealthy for the " Yankee invaders " if Old Virginia had only a " cool ten thousand" Parkers. So thinks Jim Darden, and in the conversation we hold, after Captain has left, he broadly insinuates that Robert Cannon is not as sound on State-rights doctrine as he ought to be.

"Darden," quickly replies Cannon, "whatever may be the complexion of my political principles mud and water don't change them!"

Darden recollects how he " dog-goned" the Confederacy and Jeff Davis on that stormy night-march from Culpeper, and says to his tongue " Cease firing."

At another camp-fire is assembled a mess known as the "Cockade Invincibles." Theodore Howard, or "the little corporal," is talking about the late march from Culpeper. Around him are sitting Oscar Slater, George Fowlkes, John Glenn, Andrew Harrison, John Cogbill, John James Estes, Robert Dunaway, and a number of others.

"I tell you, boys," said the loquacious little corporal, "there's plenty of red clay in Culpeper. We were slipping and floundering in it in every direction, and the darkness so great you could hardly see your hand before you. The rain coming down in torrents, horses getting stuck here and there, and the shouts of the officers summoning the cannoneers to the wheels, made it a night never to be forgotten. The caisson of my detachment missed the road, and tumbled down the hill! Then was heard the voice of the sergeant, 'Cannoneers to the wheels! Cannoneers to the wheels!' But no cannoneers were to be found! Yet those same cannoneers of the First detachment were in a few feet of their sergeant, quietly sitting under the bushes, cautioning one another in a whisper not to speak, and let some one else get into the mud and shove the caisson up the hill. After Sergeant Cogbill had shouted himself hoarse, 'Where the d——l are those cannoneers?' and getting no response, he finally went to another part of the company and got a detail of other men to extricate that caisson."

"You little rascal!" exclaimed good-natured John Estes, "I was one of that detail."

"And I too," said Fowlkes.

Little heeding these "backhanded" compliments, our "little corporal" continues his remarks.

"It was during this same night, after the caisson affair, when we had marched until about midnight— all hands being soaking wet and full of red mud— when I and several others (Aleck Williams being one) were left a little behind the command. We went to a small house on the road-side, and asked if we could be sheltered from the storm a while. A voice came from within saying, 'No; the house is full of soldiers now.' We then asked if we could find shelter in some of the out-houses? The answer was, 'No; they also are full.' Aleck Williams, being full of fun under all circumstances, and ready for any emergency, was also ready in this case of hard-hearted patriotism. So he asked, in a very loud tone of voice, 'Boys, have any of you got any matches? Let's set fire to the d——d old house!' A voice came from within promptly, saying, 'Hold on; I reckon I can find room for you.' The door was opened, and there was plenty of room for us, and for as many more, had they been there; for not a solitary soldier was in that house before we entered. We spent the balance of the night very comfortably."

"And you both should have been punished as stragglers!" laughingly said Lieutenant Brown, who, unobserved by our "little corporal," had seated himself among the "Cockade Invincibles."

Our gallant lieutenant thus got the laugh on Corporal Howard, but presently he resumed his narrative:

"You remember, lieutenant, the large number of

refugees we met as we neared Fredericksburg? They
were in all sorts of vehicles, ox-carts seeming to pre-
dominate. They were not very mild in their abuse
of the enemy, and they couldn't be blamed much
either, having been driven from their homes by a
formidable array of huge siege guns, planted above,
and aimed at their town. One old *lady* was so angry
at them as to say to me and George Jones, 'Give it
to the d——d rascals, boys, when you get there!'
We told her we would do it, which seemed to satisfy
her somewhat."

Several years ago, while residing in the city of
New York, the writer enjoyed the acquaintance of
a typical New York "boy of the period." He
flourished under the name of Arthur McGooldrick,
and was an apprentice in the *Commercial Bulletin*
office. In the employ of this office were a number
of war veterans,—all, I believe, of the South. One
day they were discussing the late war. Arthur listened. A thirst for historical knowledge was developed. Presently he came to me and said: "Mr.
Cannon, were you in that war?" "Yes," I replied.
"Was there much of a buzz about it at the time?"
I told him I thought there was. He at once resumed his work, apparently well satisfied that he
knew all that was worth knowing about the great
war between the States. You, reader, may think
our "little corporal" is "buzzing" too much, and,
as it is getting late, I will suppose that he has talked
himself tired and his comrades to sleep.

Soldier life was not without its bright side. Our

neighbors, the Washington Artillery (of New Orleans), gave a series of theatrical entertainments soon after the battle of Fredericksburg. The scene of their operations was as expansive as the most liberal poet could desire—the "wide dome of heaven," with "stars for tapers tall," around and above them, while in immediate contiguity were a number of stands piled with burning pine-knots. By this dubious light they played the "Lady of Lyons," and a young man declaimed "Bingen on the Rhine." Though during wintry weather, they played several nights to large audiences, which included some ladies from the adjacent country.

Our bugler, Eglin, was a master of the instrument, and his notes, whether calling sternly to battle or softly to sleep, linger fondly in memory; but there was a bugler in Colonel Walton's battalion who, if possible, excelled Eglin. Never can I forget the dreamy beauty of "taps" (lights out) as he played it in the pine-woods back of Fredericksburg. Sainted Leroy M. Lee loved the simile, "As soft as the notes of a flute"; but had he heard the wooing music of this "sleep call," as it floated in soothing wavelets out into the quiet woods, his gentle spirit would fain have breathed its last on the wings of such an angelus.

CHAPTER VI.

CAMP CARMEL.

"It only takes the slightest hint to send my memory roving over those dear old days, when, a parcel of beardless boys, we fought for honor and our country; for surely no one can accuse us of fighting for anything else when it took two months' pay to buy a quart of onions at the sutler's."—*Private S. P. Weisiger.*

CARMEL,—"vineyard of the LORD,"—in ancient days rich in fruitage, and still famous in poem and prophecy. "The glory of Lebanon; the excellency of Carmel and Sharon." The scene, also, of that awful prayer-test, when Elijah, the lone prophet of Truth, stood defiant before the king and priesthood of a false and idolatrous nation, and appealed to the GOD who would answer by fire! Carmel! Beautiful Carmel! Pleasant and holy are the associations that cluster, like purpling grapes, around thy sweet-sounding name!

The modern Carmel, in Syria, is sterile, and its glory is mainly of the past; but Carmel, in Caroline county, Virginia, is still more unlike it of ancient renown. Twenty years ago there stood (and probably still stands), in that county, a plain brick building known as Carmel church. The country round about is flat and sandy, and pine and cedar are the trees most common. Unlike the ancient Carmel,

too, are the associations connected with our Caroline
Carmel; for here was no terrible fire-test, but rest
after the baptism of battle; and here no treacherous
enemies, but true-hearted Southern soldiers in winter
quarters, and gentle and generous ladies to welcome
them when they went visiting in the neighborhood.
Here the boy company, and our battalion, spent the
several months intervening between the battle of
Fredericksburg and the great struggle at Chancellorsville.

Here our boys built log- and slab-houses, and fixed
themselves quite comfortably. Camp duties were
light, consisting mainly of guarding our horses and
guns, with an occasional drill or dress-parade. In
our company there was a musical club called the
"String Band." Moore, Duffey, and Hallowell, and
our bugler, Eglin, were the principal performers.
"Oft in the stilly night," when the winds were gentle,
and the moonlight shimmered through the leafless
trees, did the sweet strains of this band beguile the
earlier hours, reminding us of sweethearts and the
"old folks at home." Then, again, we would per-
petrate a desperate masculine dance to the time of
merrier strains. On Sundays, but not regularly,
there was divine service in the church near by.
The only preacher I recollect was the Rev. General
Pendleton.

All of our boys were not good boys—at least not
of the "Praise-God Barebones" type. They amused
themselves by snow-ball battles, chasing hares and
squirrels, and yelling at every citizen they saw, espe-

7

cially if he wore a tall hat, "Come down out of that hat, and join the soldier-boys, and help whip the Yanks!" The unlucky civilian is embarrassed, of course; but a hundred voices renew the cry, "Come down! Come down! I know you are up there; I see your legs!" Who would not rather face the "Yankees" than an army of such tantalizers? Thus some recruits were gained. Nor were civilians with tall hats the only victims. Sometimes a pompous or unpopular officer would receive a similar yelling salute as he came riding by. He might complain at headquarters; but how could the commanding general discipline a whole brigade for a breach of etiquette?

At this time (January, 1863) rations were sufficient, if not abundant; but, judging from the experience of Corporal Howard and his "Cockade Invincibles," they were not sufficient for their enormous appetites. Hear the "little corporal's" story:

"It was at this camp that our mess became involved in a rather serious difficulty in regard to the misappropriation (!) of a certain pig. We had drawn seven days' rations at one time. There being about a dozen of us in the mess, and all being pretty hearty eaters, in about two days the seven days' rations were all gone. After fasting a day or so, the boys began to look around the country to see what they could pick up in the way of eatables. There was an old lady, by the name of Mrs. Hacket, who lived a little way from the camp. She had a grown son, named Joe, who was a kind of an idiot. She also had some pigs. We went to her and tried to buy a pig from her; but no, she wouldn't sell one for any price. Finally Sergeant Tyler, myself, and several others picked a chance when Mrs. Hacket was absent from home, and tried our luck again. Joe Hacket being left at home alone, we tried to get one from him; but no, his mother said they must not be sold for any price. Finally Sergeant Tyler struck on a plan. It being about the time the conscription act was put in force, Tyler says, 'Boys, let's conscript the fellow and put him in the army.' All hands quickly agreed, except Joe, who became very much alarmed, and, being a large man, he violently resisted. Nevertheless he was forcibly ejected from the house, and carried over to camp, put in one of the log houses, and a mock court-martial held over him. John Pearce, acting as judge, came in with a large red blanket around him and a long knife in his hand, and took his seat opposite the prisoner. After some talk over him, he was sentenced by the judge to be taken down in the woods and hung by the neck until dead. The judge being a hard-hearted man generally, we were not surprised at his decision. To carry out the sentence we got a prolong, or rope, from one of the guns, carried poor Joe down in a bottom in the depths of the woods, out of reach of the officers; put the rope around his neck, threw it over the limb of a tree, and began to pull away on poor Joe. After getting him up on his toes, he begging most pitifully all the time, Bill Mays asked him would he let us have a pig now? Yes, we could have them all,

if we would let him down—might have everything
he had.   Some one asked him for his pocket-book;
but he didn't have one.   He was then let down,
being more scared than hurt; for we didn't intend to
hurt the poor fellow, but simply to scare the pig
out of him.   We then followed him home.   He
jumped in the pen, and insisted on our taking all
the pigs.   We told him no; that one would do.   We
took the pig, carried him over to camp, killed him,
and cooked him, and that night made a big eat of
pig meat without bread.   I think we cleaned the
whole of that pig up that night before retiring.
Some other men in camp being acquainted with
Mrs. Hacket, and also friendly towards her, told her
the names of those connected with the pig scrape,
and she reported the facts to Colonel Alexander.
The next day orders came to camp to put Sergeant
Tyler, Corporal Howard, and the rest of the pig
men under guard, which order was promptly put
into effect, and the whole party was court-martialed.
The officers of the court-martial laughed heartily
as the trial proceeded.   Their decision was read out
at dress-parade, and when the order was given,
'Battalion!   Right face, break ranks, march!'   I
reckon there never was such a grunting and squeal-
ing heard before as that battalion set up!   The pig
men quickly disappeared from the view of these un-
kind grunters.   Their punishment was double duty
for the privates and a public reprimand to the non-
commissioned officers."

Snow-ball battles were sometimes fought with

such vigor as to disable the combatants. The result of such a fight was the capture of the defeated party's cooking utensils, and any food that might be contained in them.

Whilst at this camp we drew for rations most excellent beef, but not a great quantity of it, three or four men sharing among themselves about as much as one ought to have. The mess was a soldier family. Having to cook, eat, and sleep together, they naturally had their little contentions. Two members of a certain mess, whom we shall call Bill and Tom, raised a row about a very simple matter. The question was whether the gravy should be thickened. Bill wanted it thickened; but Tom did not. The dispute waxed hot. Pending differences between the Confederacy and the United States were forgotten, for a while at least, until this question could be settled. Bill had been in the habit of having his way about things generally, but this time Tom swore he would have his way. They finally came to blows. Then one threw the other down, rolled each other over and over in the ashes, kicked over the pan of gravy, and were only separated after the day's rations were lost. The result was the whole mess had to fast the balance of the day!

In our battalion was a company familiarly known as the "Madison Tips." The name will be recognized by all old soldiers of the Army of Northern Virginia; for the thunder of their big guns was heard in every battle. They were recruited from Louisiana and Mississippi, and were mostly brawny

Irishmen. Captain Moody, their commander, was one of the handsomest men in the army. When we invaded Pennsylvania the people would have it that he was General Lee. The "Tips" were splendid fighting men. When their battery of 24-pounders opened on the enemy he was forcibly reminded that the "Tips" had introduced themselves for the express purpose of business. They were a set of men that seemed born for the purpose of fighting, and when they could not get up a fight with the "Yanks" would often raise a fight among themselves—mostly for the fun of it, it appeared—and did actually sometimes kill one another. Although uncouth in exterior, and nearly all of them carrying a butcher-knife buckled to the waist, they were kind-hearted when they "took a liking" to any one. "I have had them to come to me many a time on long marches," says our little Corporal Howard, "and take my baggage off my back and carry it for me, with the remark, 'Sure and you are too small to be carrying that: let me carry it for you.'" It may easily be imagined that these fierce, restless men were often the subjects of discipline. They were not noted for scrupulous regard for the rights of private property, and availed themselves of any shallow pretext to "appropriate" it. Says Corporal Howard: "They would not allow a cow to gore or a hog to bite them, and if either animal attempted such a thing it would be most unceremoniously transferred to their huge camp kettles and ovens, which they never failed to retain on the march, no matter what else was lost or left behind.

A cow or hog in the immediate vicinity of their camp stood little or no show whatever." Eatables were not the only objects of their covetousness. These fiery spirits were fond of "fire water." As we were to have our quarters at Carmel for the winter, Lieutenant Smith was sent out to explore the neighborhood for whiskey, etc., so that it might not fall into the hands of the " Tips," or any of the rest of us. After establishing the quarters of the battalion officers in a school-house, the lieutenant appeared with two barrels of whiskey. It was decided that the best place to store it was in this same school-house. This house was of wood, and raised from the ground on pine stumps, about two feet in front and probably three feet in rear, as the ground was sloping. From the door in front to the back of the house there was a wide passage, on each side of which were two rooms occupied by the battalion officers. The barrels were placed in the passage, and a sentinel posted near them. Of course the whiskey was safe now ! But the " Tips " had made up their minds to have it. One bright, frosty morning the air around the school-house was odorous of whiskey. What was the matter ? Had the hoops broken ? So it would seem, for the floor was flooded with the fiery fluid. An inspection was made. A hole had been bored through the floor into one of the barrels, and the "Tips " had taken the contents out by buckets full !

Captain Moody was killed soon after the war—it was reported, by his own men.

As I have never seen any account in print of a
performance familiarly known among soldiers as

" RUNNING THE BLOCK,"

(blockade,) I have concluded to relate under this
head an adventure which was of thrilling interest to
three members of the boy battery. These were
David Brown, Robert Cannon, and Marion Francisco.
The company had passed through two arduous and
sanguinary campaigns, and was now resting. Both
Federals and Confederates were in winter quarters.
It was natural that we should think about home and
furloughs; yet no furloughs came. We longed with
youthful fondness for a sight of the dear faces of
relatives and friends. This longing finally grew
into a passionate determination on the part of these
three men to go home at all hazards, if but to stay a
day or two. The distance to Richmond was about
thirty miles.

At dusk one cold January evening they started on
their hazardous tramp. They were committing an
offence for which men, actuated by motives perhaps
equally as pure as their own, had suffered death at
the hands of inexorable courts-martial. But of this
they thought not. The army was quiet; they intended to return in a few days; home-sickness was
preying upon their unsophisticated hearts, and "On
to Richmond" was the watchword of the night.

There is no moon—only starlight; and the ground
is frozen and the night air nipping cold. We are
now walking rapidly down the old "Telegraph"

road. Conscious of doing wrong, every unusual
sound startles us, and all wagon-camps on the road-
side are carefully flanked. Mile after mile is noiselessly traversed.

At last, about two hours after midnight, we are
within five miles of Richmond. We have walked
about twenty-five miles. Tired and perplexed, we sit
down under a cedar-tree to rest and plan. Between
us and the city we know there is a cordon of pickets,
but at what particular points they are stationed we
are not certain.

We start again, marching warily. To be detected
now would not only be death to the hope of seeing
our homes, but expose us to the tender mercies of
the hated provost authorities at Richmond.

The four-mile stone is passed, and we are quietly
pressing on, when, lo! we suddenly find ourselves
within a few yards of a sentry-box!

"Bob, step softly," whispered David Brown, and
our hearts beat quicker than our footsteps.

The sentinel is in his box, and we may yet pass
unobserved.

Just as we arrive in front of the box there is an
ominous stir within, and presently we hear what
may be the words of doom:

"Halt! Who goes there?"

"Friends!" answers Cannon, with affected bold-
ness.

"Have you got a pass?"

"Yes; do you want to see it," replies Cannon, who
has in his pocket a wretchedly forged slip that would

double his punishment in the Confederate " Castle Thunder," if inspected by a practised eye.

" All right, gentlemen; pass on," are the welcome words we next hear.

" Here's the pass, if you want to see it," impudently insists Cannon.

" Yes; show it to him, Bob ! " chimes in David Brown.

" Never mind, gentlemen ; pass on ! " replies the unsuspicious sentinel. And we pass !

About four o'clock that (Sunday) morning Robert Cannon knocked at the back door of his mother's residence in the east end of Richmond, having walked more than thirty miles. He was soon in the tender embraces of his mother, with brother and sister lovingly near. There was a cloud on their faces when he told them of the illicit manner of his visit ; but he was still a dear boy, and had seen danger and hardship; and mother-love condones all things.

At nine o'clock he was promptly in his place in Union Methodist Sunday-school, as "fresh as a daisy." But " daisies" were not in season; and the kindly greetings of pastor and teacher and schoolmates were not in unison with the voice of Duty, which sternly whispered, " Your place is at Camp Carmel."

In the meanwhile we were missed at camp, and Lieutenant Brown, commanding the battery, had telegraphed to the Richmond authorities to have us arrested.

David Brown quietly returned to camp on the third day after our long tramp. Cannon and Francisco decided to linger one day more amidst the attractions of the city, and this delay doomed them to another and not less hazardous adventure than the night walk from Caroline county.

On this last day as Robert Cannon, escorted by his brother Baylor, was walking along one of the retired streets of the city, they were met by a stranger, who civilly accosted them, and inquired if they knew where Mr. Cannon resided?

"Which Mr. Cannon?" quickly asked Robert's brother.

"Mr. Robert Cannon," answered the stranger.

At this moment Robert suspected who the stranger was and what he wanted, and tried to signal Baylor to that effect; but in vain, for Baylor immediately responded—

"Here is Mr. Robert Cannon!"

The stranger was detective Craddock, of General Winder's city forces, and had an order to arrest Robert, which he accordingly did, and took him to the headquarters of Major Griswold, one of Winder's assistants.

In the meantime Francisco was arrested, and both he and Cannon were arraigned before Griswold. It was decided that Cannon should make the defence, if they were allowed to answer for themselves.

They did not wait long before their turn for trial arrived. "Justice" was terribly quick in this military court. The charge against them was "absence

without leave," and Robert plead "guilty." He
was proceeding tremblingly to state some facts that
might palliate the offence, and was just beginning
probably the second or third sentence of his timid
speech with the phrase "I think," when—

"Think!" thundered the military judge, "a soldier has no right to think!"

A little girl was once asked the question, "What
is the soul?" to which she replied, "It is my think!"
According to this definition, people with souls cannot make good soldiers! Surely, thought we, there
are no "inalienable" rights, and "liberty" and
"happiness" are pursued under insuperable difficulties!

Without further ado, Cannon and Francisco were
sentenced to Castle Booker—a dirty prison, where
vermin thrived and men languished, and over whose
entrance might be truly inscribed, "He who enters
here leaves self-respect behind."

While all this was going on in the court room
Baylor Cannon was actively working outside. He
found Captain Parker, who happened to be in the
city. Just as the prisoners were about to be sent
to the miserable "Castle," in walked Baylor and the
Captain. A few words passed between our commander and the judge, and the prisoners were free!
Trusting to their honor, Captain Parker gave them
permission to go where they chose until the next
day, when they voluntarily and unguarded returned
to camp. There they were subjected to the mild
punishment of a public lecture on the turpitude of

their offence, and three weeks' "double duty," with *banishment from camp.*

This "banishment" from camp was the beginning of one of the most pleasant episodes of my soldier life. The tents of the "banished" men were pitched in a pine woods where the horses were kept. When "off duty" (guarding cannon) we diverted ourselves in various ways, and with much greater freedom than if we were under the immediate eye of the officers in the soldier-city near the church. It was not our duty, but we chose to assist the drivers in "watering" the horses. Each one was careful to ride slowly and demurely until safely out of sight of official critics, when, presto! we rode as gaily and swiftly as the mettle of our steeds permitted. Not content with going an unnecessarily long distance to water the horses, one day Tucker and I made a detour in the direction of a handsome farm-house. Riding boldly up to the front entrance, we dismounted and introduced ourselves to its inmates. These were two ladies, Mrs. Bettie Dickinson and Miss Julia Winston, who received us so civilly that we were encouraged to linger perhaps an hour and converse freely.

During the conversation Mrs. Dickinson alluded to the unprotected condition of her residence and farm. Her husband, Dr. Sam. Dickinson, was on duty as surgeon in a Richmond hospital, and could make only short visits to his country home. There were some unscrupulous marauders among the troops encamped in the neighborhood, and she wished to

secure the services of two gentlemanly soldiers as
guards. Tucker and I were more than willing to
assume this pleasant duty; but, alas! we were under
the ban for at least a week to come. We told Mrs.
Dickinson that just then circumstances embarrassed
us; but if she could only wait awhile, we would be
most happy to serve her. Sure enough, in about a
week, Tucker and I were ordered to report at Dr.
Dickinson's as guards.

"Guard duty" at Dr. Dickinson's, as we had an-
ticipated, was remarkably pleasant. We had all the
comforts of a home. Of course, the barns and premises generally were inspected at night; but seldom
was our rest disturbed after we once retired to our
comfortable bed. Tucker, however, much to his
disgust, was recalled to camp, and Charlie Murray
took his place.

Charlie Murray was the "dude" of the battalion.
His face was of almost feminine beauty—a rosy dark
complexion, black eyes, and luxuriant black hair;
small of stature, but strong and agile. His success
in keeping neat and nice in dress was the subject of
marvel among his comrades. When others were
not able to maintain a simply healthful cleanliness,
Murray would appear with spotless collar and shining shoes, and his whole attire as presentable as the
utmost care could make it. Was he a good soldier?
Yes; "womanish" men often have truer courage
than the rough people who pick their teeth with
bowie-knives.

One of our pleasant duties was to escort the ladies

in their visits in the neighborhood. Mounted on good horses, and visiting among the best people in Caroline, we had a time that was doubtless much envied by our less fortunate comrades.

Murray and I had been "guarding" this pleasant residence a month or more when Captain Parker conceived the idea that we were having too easy a time. He ordered us back to camp, and two other men were sent in our place. This did not suit Mrs. Dickinson, and we had been in camp only a few days when an order came from General Alexander that Cannon and Murray must report at once for guard duty at Dr. Dickinson's. Thus our would-be impartial Captain was worsted by a woman's wit.

Never can I forget some of the home scenes at this residence. The Doctor would come up from Richmond about once a week. He was a fine-looking man, of perhaps thirty-five years, polished in manners, and could sing, as well as play on several instruments. In the long winter evenings, while a wood-fire blazed on the ample hearth, with his wife and Miss Winston, and Murray and I seated comfortably around, the Doctor would "tune up" his guitar and sing such sweet old love songs as "Come, dearest, the daylight is gone," and "Annie Laurie," or perhaps some merrier but equally pure-spirited words. It was the poetry of home life. He impressed me as one of the few married men who carried into the "holy estate" that sweetness of demeanor that makes up the bliss of courtship, and too often ends with it.

The author of the following lines must have had some such scene in his mind when he wrote—

> "Oh, there's a power to make each hour
> As sweet as Heaven designed it;
> Nor need we roam to bring it home,
> Though few there be that find it!
>
> We seek too high for things close by,
> And lose what nature found us;
> For life has here no charm so dear
> As home and friends around us."

Whilst my heart is full of "love, rest, and home," let me describe my "Nellie Gray." I can do so all the more frankly because she married somebody else, and twenty and five years have added silver to our locks if not to our pockets, assuaged my griefs and given her a happy home and children. War-beaten Richmond was her home. I knew her from a child, and loved her with a boy's romantic but bashful ardor. It was not a mere fancy. She was really beautiful and good. Black hair and dark-brown eyes, and a complexion not too fair, but rich in rosy health. Soft was her voice, and her demeanor gentle. The sweetest of our south-winds loved to linger in the tresses of her flowing hair. Like another simple lover, I never told my love; but, unlike her, "concealment" did no injury to my "damask cheek." In fact, my "cheek" was not of the "damask" variety. It led me, with Parker, to seek the "field of glory," and stand up for brave Richmond and—beautiful EMMA.

But she married the other fellow!

A remarkable feature in Mrs. Dickinson's character was the pronounced distinction she always made in favor of the private soldier. Some ladies were only gracious to those on whose coat-collars glittered a "star" or more. Not thus our fair hostess. If a distinction must be made, it should be in favor of the untitled patriot. Well do I recollect the lesson she taught me on this point. Two divisions of the First corps were marching down the road past the residence. The weather was rainy and cold. Some of these troops encamped for a night near the house. Mrs. Dickinson was very hospitable and patriotic, and she instructed me to give food and shelter to as many soldiers as possible. Before bed-time that night every spare space in the mansion was taken, and even the out-houses were filled with soldiers. It was when there was really no room for any more that General Wilcox applied for quarters. I was embarrassed. How could I refuse quarters to a Major-General? In this dilemma I went to Mrs. Dickinson.

"You know, Mr. Cannon," said she quietly, "that the house is filled up, and we can't possibly take in any more."

"But, Mrs. Dickinson," I urged, "he is a Major-General!"

"Mr. Cannon, I am astonished at you, sir! You ought to know me better than that!"

The look and tone with which she said these words were enough for me, and I firmly informed "the General" that he could not be accommodated.

8

With balmy spring and "the singing of birds" came marching orders. Other than the sights and sounds of nature and a pleasant home were to engage our attention. Miss Winston, at parting, gave me a small-print Bible—such I as could conveniently carry on the march. I put it in my jacket pocket— just over my heart. It would serve to stop a bullet. Besides, I had a just veneration for the sacred thing, and an adoring respect for the truths therein contained. I have that Bible now. On its fly-leaf might be written a long list of battles in which the boy company was engaged, from that sunny April day when I received it, to another April day, two years thereafter, when, weary and wasted, we surrendered to "overwhelming numbers and resources." It could whisper of the thunders of Gettysburg, and chaunt with tortuous Chicamauga the requiem of the dead. It could tell of tears and prayer, amidst hunger and nakedness, heart-sickness and weariness, endured for honor and country's sake. But more—infinitely more—it might tell of battles since the war!—of struggles with self and sin—of conflicts, not against mere flesh and blood, but "against principalities, against powers, against the rulers of the darkness of this world, against spiritual wickedness in high places"! God omnipotent forbid that there should be an Appomattox as the conclusion to this tremendous conflict, with the black flag of Evil floating forever over us!

Forever? Yes; F O R E V E R!

CHAPTER VII.

MARYE'S HILL AND CHANCELLORSVILLE.

"The boy battery was always one of my favorites."—General E. P. Alexander.

A RE there any Virginians in this party?"
The speaker was a well dressed citizen, and he asked the question of a lot of Confederate prisoners standing in line in Washington city.

"No, sir; they don't stand long enough to be captured!"

This answer was given by a man standing close by me, and so quickly that for a moment I was abashed. I faced him at once, and told him he lied. He knew it, the impudent fool, and quailed. He had the honor to belong to the far-famed Washington Artillery, of New Orleans.

The first section of the Parker Battery, under Lieutenant J. Thompson Brown, were prisoners of war. The story of their capture I will tell.

On or about May 1, 1863, near Chancellorsville, Lieutenant Brown was ordered to take the men and and horses—not guns—of the first section of the Parker Battery, and report to General Barksdale, at Fredericksburg.

On the way I saw Stonewall Jackson for the last

time. He conversed with our Lieutenant for a few minutes.

Arriving at Fredericksburg, Lieutenant Brown received orders to relieve an officer commanding two Parrott guns in redoubts on the extreme right of Marye's Hill. These orders called for the delivery of the guns to Brown and his men. The officer objected: it was an implied slur on his capacity or courage. But the orders were imperative, and, actually shedding tears, he reluctantly surrendered his guns to us.

Brown made us a little speech, in which he told us that we came there to win or die, and that Gen. Alexander had selected us because he knew we could be trusted.

Things did look serious. We had a strong position, it is true, with the prestige of victory—and on that very spot—in our favor. The Federals had good reason to dread the grey stone wall at the foot of the hill. In our front is the "dark and bloody ground" in which so many of them found a sepulchre last December.

It is Saturday, the second day of May. Our men are idly lounging about the guns, which are placed in earthworks. Lieutenant Brown is sitting on the incline of the hill, just beyond the works. He is singing in a low tone, and tapping his boot's toe in time with the tune. I can catch only a word or two of the gentle ditty. It is something about capturing a fair lady. The song is evidently of love, and not of war. The Lieutenant is newly married !

The scene before him is one of romantic beauty. The field beyond the stone wall is bathed in the flood of yellow glory that pours from an unclouded sun, and the Rappahannock glances back in gladness, while, beyond all, the heights of Stafford rise "tall and divinely fair."

There was a saying among the men, "Why, soldiers, why should we be melancholy, whose business 'tis to die?" But dying is a melancholy business!

Verdure, and glancing river, and towering heights are not all that the eye can see. Twenty-thousand Federals, under General Sedgwick, are preparing to attack our position, and General Early has scarcely three thousand men to resist them. On Marye's Hill (that is, the present cemetery portion) there are only four pieces of artillery—our two, and the two to our left under Captain Squires. At the foot of the hill are about five hundred infantry, under General Wm. Barksdale. They are Mississippians, and will "do to tie to."

General Sedgwick is maturing his plans and marshalling his forces to take this position. If he can do it, he can get in Lee's rear at Chancellorsville; and what then?

On this Saturday afternoon, of the second day of May, even a short-sighted private can see enough to make him feel insecure. What can this handful of Confederates, however devoted and brave, do against the overwhelming numbers that are about to be hurled against them?

At night-fall we quietly limber up our pieces, and retire from the hill. It looks like a retreat, and retreat seems to be the only course open. We go perhaps two miles up the road when we meet some infantry coming to our assistance. Cheer after cheer breaks the stillness of the woods, and we at once return to the redoubts on Marye's hill. It seems that the enemy did not discover our absence, for we resume our former position without opposition. Then we are ordered to collect brush-wood and build big fires. Soon the whole hill is aglare. The night, however, is warm, and the fires soon die out; and the enemy make the inference that we are very weak. The fires were built to impress them differently; but the trick was " too thin."

"The night before the battle!" What thrilling associations cluster around these words in the soldier's heart! The solemn, circling stars, and perhaps the moon gleaming through half-concealing clouds, shining alike upon far-away home and its devoted defender; the rustling leaves just in front, perhaps moved by the winds, perhaps by the tread of a stealthy foe; and then the flash of the picket-gun, and the quick, resounding report, which tells that the enemy are not all asleep!

As we lay down to sleep we can hear the cannonading which even night does not stop at Chancellorsville. The drowsy imagination pictures fierce demons flinging thunderbolts in the air, as the great, swelling sounds seem to collide and intermingle, advance and recede. Then all is quiet, or we are very tired, and the soldier-boy sleeps as sweetly as when his mother watched by his cradle, and hymned gentle songs of peace and heaven.

At dawn of Sunday, May 3d, we are standing by our two guns. Sergeant James M. Tyler has charge of one, and Sergeant Wm. B. Cogbill of the other, with Corporals Sam. Duffey, Phil. Scherer, and Wm. Verlander to assist them. Including all, cannoneers and drivers, Lieut. Brown has about forty men.

During the night the enemy had posted three batteries in our front, and now they open on us fiercely. Brown's orders are to reserve his fire for infantry only; but the fire of these batteries is so severe, and we are losing horses so rapidly, that he determines to return it. But what are our two guns against a battalion? He goes to Squires, on our left, and begs him to "divide fire" with him—that is, to open on the Federal batteries and thus attract a part of this leaden storm to himself. Squires declines, pleading his orders to fire at infantry only.

Our horses are protected by the rise of the hill; but, notwithstanding this, every few minutes we hear the cry, "Lieutenant, another horse killed!"

This tempest of cannon-shot is preliminary to the infantry charge of the Federals. And see! they come, in apparently overwhelmingly numbers. Their lines move rapidly towards our right and rear. Our guns are now forced to "take" the fire of the batteries, and give all their attention to the infantry. The Mississippians stand firmly behind the stone wall, and fire with deadly accuracy, while the guns on the hill blaze faster and faster. The enemy is repulsed. Again they charge, and are again driven back.

General Sedgwick, in his official report, acknowledged that he lost "a thousand men killed in ten minutes."

Our Lieutenant is painfully wounded and stunned temporarily by a cannon-shot, but recovers sufficiently to stand to his post.

About 11 o'clock a white flag is displayed by the enemy. There is brief cessation of hostilities, while Colonel Griffin, of the Mississippians, receives the men who bring it. There is a parley, and the men with the white flag return to the Federal lines.

But they had seen our weakness, and soon after our reception of their truce-flag they make another effort. In front we repulse them, as before; but behold! a rapidly advancing column on our left, sweeping down from the direction of the Marye house!

"Hurrah, boys, here comes reinforcements!" says somebody.

"Reinforcements, the devil! They are Yankees!" says Cogbill.

Squires' guns are already taken, and those are hostile bayonets gleaming on our left flank!

We pull our gun out of the redoubt to fire on this new foe, leaving only Tyler's gun to face the enemy in front.

Rapidly Cogbill's gun is shotted with canister. No. 4 (John Hightower), with lanyard firmly grasped, asks quickly, "Billy, must I fire?"

The enemy is almost on us, and it looks like madness to fire now.

"Fire!" says Cogbill.

This discharge, at such close quarters, kills a number of our assailants, and for a moment they waver; but they are soon among us, and we are prisoners. They kill one of our men (Ed. Martin) after he has surrendered; but, it is hoped, not through malice. They seem to be more scared than we are, and some of them seem to be half drunk. They fire wildly. One or two of our men (John Thomas Williams and Turner) escape during this exciting mixing of blue jackets with gray.

As the stars and stripes are planted on our works, one of our boys says to Sergeant Cogbill, "Billy, isn't that a beautiful flag?"

"Where is the officer commanding these guns?" demands a Major of the Sixth Maine infantry, mounted on a black horse.

"I have that honor," answers Lieutenant Brown. As he says these words he raises his hat, expecting a bullet in reply.

The generous Federal, however, strongly compliments us for our pluck and endurance, and details Captain ——, with some men of Company "A," to escort us to the rear. Lieutenant Brown cannot forget the kindness of this officer, for they spent more than an hour together on the field, where they met General Sedgwick, who took occasion to compliment the TWO guns which contended with his batteries.

The famous hill is taken, but not until General

Lee has whipped General Hooker at Chancellorsville; and, though now prisoners of war, we have accomplished the purpose in view—held back Sedgwick's corps, which will soon be driven over the river by our victorious comrades pouring down from Chancellorsville.

The loss in our band of forty is only one man killed (Martin) and several wounded. In fact, the situation called more for fortitude than courage, as we were well protected by earthworks; but for which, and the good providence of GOD, many of us would have shared the fate of our horses, nearly all of which were killed. "When a man's right," said a bluff Virginia farmer, "he's powerful hard to hit." So say I, too; but I would feel easier if good earthworks are added to the triple armor of a just cause.

We were treated very courteously by our captors, and in three weeks were exchanged and back with Parker and the boy battery, ready to dance in the next ball of the military season—Gettysburg.

Would that my work as historian of the boy company could end with this simple narrative of duty done; but it is my unpleasant task to right a wrong, even if in so doing I should pluck a feather from the cap of "the South's most celebrated battalion of artillery"—the "Washington," of New Orleans. For years the part that Brown and his men played on the famous hill has been quietly ignored; but latterly this battalion, not content with an already redundant newspaper glory, has stretched its covetous hand to tear from the helmet of the boy company an honor which it fairly won and—deserves to wear.

It seems that General Fitz. Lee, in his lecture on " Chancellorsville," failed to mention the Washington Artillery. When the lecture was delivered in New Orleans, in April, 1883, this omission was noticed, and caused marked dissatisfaction among the members and friends of that battalion. Said a New Orleans newspaper:

"Any account of the tremendous battles of Fredericksburg and Chancellorsville that should fail to mention that heroic and historic command whose splendid deeds have illuminated the pages of American history, and shed an undying lustre on this city and State, would be singularly lacking in accuracy and completeness. Never were guns better manned; never was the slaughter of artillery fire more terrible; and no mention of Fredericksburg nor Marye's Heights can ever be made without calling up instantly glorious memories of the South's most celebrated battalion of artillery."

This newspaper then gives details of how " Sedgwick's command of 24,000 men was held in check by Barksdale's brigade of 1,400 men, Hays' Louisiana brigade, a Mississippi brigade, and—the Washington Artillery (!), in all not exceeding 3,000 men, during the battle of Chancellorsville, thus determining the main issue in that battle."

In a letter to the editor of the *City Item*, dated June 1, 1883, General Lee apologizes for this omission, saying: "In my address on Chancellorsville I dealt more particularly with Jackson's flank march and attack on the enemy. The guns of the Washington Artillery did not participate in that movement, but were left behind, under Early, near Fredericksburg, and fought with their accustomed dash and courage against Sedgwick."

Surely this explanation would seem to be sufficient; but not in the hypercritical judgment of the admirers of "the South's most celebrated battalion."

If the Washington Artillery is really aggrieved by Gen. Lee's failure to laud it in his lecture, surely the veterans of the boy company can sympathize with them; for it seems we are to go down in history (!) as members of "the South's most celebrated battalion." No mention of Brown and his forty men is made whatever; but the "tremendous" engagement is fought by the small force of infantry and—the Washington Artillery! The battalion successively commanded by S. D. Lee, E. P. Alexander, and Frank Huger fought often side by side with the "most celebrated" command of Walton, but never hoped to rank as an integral part thereof. Surely that was an honor to which, even in its wildest yearnings after "bubble reputation," it scarcely dared to aspire. But "some have greatness thrust upon them," and Brown and his men, who were the first to fire and the last to be silent on the 3d of May, 1863, in the "tremendous" engagement with Sedgwick, may strut in history as heroes of matchless prowess—only, they must recollect that they are

Washington Artillery! Be sure, boys, to recollect
your new name. You might forget, and babble the
name of Parker or Brown, of George Saville or
Leonidas Tucker, and then your bubble reputation
would burst!

There are other Richmond batteries that may
fairly share in these pseudonymic glories. The
"Crenshaw," at Sharpsburg, and the "Fayette,"
when it supplied a certain "rifle section" at Drew-
ry's Bluff, were complimented as "Washington"
artillery; and Clopton and Harry Jones, McCann
and Allegre, Ellett and the Youngs are heroes all—
under the name of "Washington" artillery!

Say, "most celebrated" gentlemen, what were
you doing on that stormy Sunday morning? If
"lightning scorched the very ground beneath your
feet," where was the thunder? Lightnings did flash
keen and quick on the historic heights, and were followed by "tremendous" roarings. Why were you
so modestly silent? Ah! we have it now: You
furnished lightning and we supplied thunder. Of
course, you do not "steal our thunder." It is only
a case of what Corporal Howard terms "misappropriation."

It may be conceded that there are good reasons
why the "most celebrated battalion" has grown so
huge in martial stature. If "the pen is mightier
than the sword," these elegant warriors have had
the full benefit of that adjunct to military fame; and
the pencil of the artist as well. In *Harpers' Weekly*
for May 23, 1863, appeared an illustration of the

"capture of the heights of Fredericksburg, by the Sixth Maine regiment, of Sedgwick's corps." Among other things pictured are two "rebel" cannon, and one of them is badly battered. These are designated by the *Weekly* as "Washington Artillery"! We cannot blame our late comrades much for quietly allowing artist and editor thus to increase their celebrity. Human nature in general is "celebrated" for its weakness. It is easy for the rich to get richer; and if the poor will persist in sending them presents, it might be discourteous to decline the gifts. Nor was the saying a mere witticism that the late war in this country was "a little difficulty between the United States and the Washington Artillery." There are skeptical people, however, who insist that the infantry, and even the "buttermilk rangers," had "a hand in that fight." But in the roar of the big guns the musketry could scarcely be heard, and in the smoke of conflict the flash of the sabre might be too dim to be seen. Conceding that the big guns scared people tremendously, did not the Otey, the Hampden, the Thomas, the Fayette, the Purcell, the Crenshaw, and the three "Howitzer" batteries—all "Richmonds in the field"—assist a little? May not Pegram, Johnson, Cabell, Brander, Stanard, Macon, Courtney, Walker, and others claim some crumbs at the banquet of honor? Did not one of the batteries under Alexander *relieve* some Washington artillery at Fredericksburg when the "most celebrated" had run —out of ammunition?

It is not the purpose of the writer to do injustice

to the reputation of our late comrades—especially not to their gallant dead, who sleep on so many battlefields; but the Crescent City soldiers, while doing well and worthily, should not arrogate to themselves all the honors, nor indulge too freely in the superlative degree of comparison. If they insist upon being "the most celebrated," we may concede it; but "most celebrated" for what?

Ah me! what a pity it is that heroes cannot be their own historians! What a pity it is they cannot attend their own funerals? How grandly would the "Old Guard" of Napoleon, or the patriot-martyrs of Thermopylæ step forth in martial procession, while Music thrilled the trembling air, and Beauty waved her loveliest honors! But, alas! the real heroes died for the "bubble reputation," and cannot (at least to mortal vision) be present at these grand obsequies.

The plain, "solid-shot" truth is that the fight with Sedgwick was not very sanguinary. General Barksdale, in his official report, says that he was assaulted by three lines of battle, twenty thousand strong, and the enemy as twenty against one. "A more heroic struggle was never made," he says, "by a mere handful of men against overwhelming odds." Yet the enemy had a discreet fear of the grim stone wall and the cannon-crowned heights that had been so fatal to Burnside, and charged rather timidly. They could not have come "to do or die," or twenty thousand men would have made the tour of the heights at the first effort. The fire of the Federal batteries was accurate and energetic; but our earth-works were an effective barrier to deadly execution. What was done by the Confederate artillery was mainly, if not entirely, done by the four guns under Brown and Squires, and it is hoped that "history" will not rob them of their laurels.

CHANCELLORSVILLE.

At the last roll-call pending the battle of Chancellorsville Captain Parker made a brief address to the boys, in which he urged that "if we win this fight, it will be the last of the war." This assurance was growing monotonous, as our sanguine Captain had said something similar on the eve of other battles.

As the "historian" of the boy company was one of those who went with Brown to Fredericksburg, he could not possibly, even with the most liberal stretch of historical license, be present also at Chancellorsville. The following account, therefore, is from other pens. With Parker is left only two guns. To assist him there is Saville and Wooldridge, lieutenants, and Ed. Moore and Joshua Hallowell, sergeants, with John Cogbill, Tom Todd, Sam Weisiger, George Jones, Frank Turnley, Hancock, and a number of other gay and gallant boys who are anxious to follow where their commander leads.

Presently the word was sounded, "Limber to the front," and we began the glad advance. We had here rather a good joke upon our Captain. In the rapid advance on the enemy, who was already retreating, one of the guns got from under his eye, and was ordered by General Jackson to move at a gallop, and take a position yet nearer to the enemy. Presently, missing the gun, Captain Parker, with flushed face and in no good humor, put spurs to his horse, and, overtaking the flying artillery, demanded in an angry tone—

"Sergeant, where are you carrying that gun? Halt!"

The sergeant, without halting in the least, replied:

"I am under General Jackson's orders, sir."

Seeing the General close to the gun, the Captain "subsided," and cried out with the best grace he could, "Forward!"

The "Catarpin" road was now clear of the enemy, and General Jackson soon commenced his great flank movement which resulted so disastrously to Hooker's army.

It was just before sunset when we again came by this great detour into the Plank road, and, after advancing a little down the road, saw one or two regiments of the enemy moving rapidly in retreat. Our infantry had got at them. They were nearly, if not quite a mile off, but we gave them a few shots to help them on.

Just after dark we heard, some hundreds of yards in our front, quite a volley from the infantry. It proved to be the most important and the saddest volley fired during the whole war. By it was slain, with brother hand, the great STONEWALL—a real

9

pillar of strength. A sad and dreary silence followed that musketry. It was "prophetic of an end." How often that day, seated on his horse, had I heard him say to courier after courier, who came at full gallop with reports from the front, simply— "Drive them! Drive them!"

And they were driven, and driven; and would have been driven into the Rappahannock but for this sad event.

At 4 o'clock next morning we were ready to move, rejoicing in the prospect of seeing the enemy's back as well as his front. We moved down the road towards Chancellorsville (which had been taken in rear), and soon came up with some of the members of our battalion, who informed us that the rest of the command was a little ahead. Soon Col. Alexander rode up to the Captain and ordered him to advance down the road till he reached an old tavern. Before we got to the tavern, however, the enemy began to throw shells thick and fast right down the road, and caused quite a "ducking" among officers and men.

After halting an hour or so at this tavern (there was nothing to drink in it!) the battalion proceeded slowly along the road, hearing pretty heavy infantry firing on our right. Halting in a pine thicket in our front, we soon were satisfied that presently there would be "something for every man to do." A heavy engagement was going on just in our front beyond the pine thicket.

At a point where roads intersect sits General Lee

on his horse, grandly calm. As the battalion dashes past, he lifts his hat. "Robert, it was the proudest moment of my life," says enthusiastic little Sam. Weisiger.

There is among officers and men a solemnity just before an engagement which is peculiar. All feel that the hour is a solemn one. The silence is often broken by a whistle or a laugh or joke, but it is all evidently forced. It, however, has its uses. It diverts the mind, for a time at least, from gloomy apprehensions. It is almost too late for the unprepared to get ready for death, and, as every one expects that not himself but his neighbor will be hit, the disposition to real, hearty reformation of life is not sound and effectual. These moments of "waiting to go in" are equal to a half hour of real fighting. In the fight the mind is intensely engaged and the hands busy. The face is flushed and the blood boiling through the arteries. All is action! action! action! Those who are really cowards by nature (and some doubtless are) become almost paralyzed, and stand (if they can stand) with their knees smiting together, and their eyes sometimes deeply sunken in their sockets, and in other cases almost popping out of their heads. In the engagement which I am about to describe, a conscript, lately enlisted—a tall, gawky youth of twenty-one from a neighboring county—was directed by the Captain to hold the horses to one of the caissons, as they were very restive. The Captain was also satisfied he would go to the rear if not watched. While attempting to take hold of the reins with trembling hands, he said, between chattering teeth: "Captain—C-a-p-t-a-i-n ! Don't you think I do m-i-g-h-t-y w-e-l-l for the first f-i-g-h-t !"

But to return. Presently the Colonel and battery commanders were seen to mount their horses. We heard the solemn words, Attention ! Mount ! Forward ! and we move towards the pine thicket, beyond which the firing was now terrific. Our comrades are in deadly conflict, and we go to join the carnival of death. "Forward ! Forward ! Drive up your horses !" The men, at a trot, follow in silence, close to their guns. Few words are spoken. No. 4 feels for his lanyard; No. 3 for his priming wire. Soon we reach the woods, and soon we see, or imagine, what awaits us beyond the gloomy thicket. Men by the dozen, some with broken arms or bleeding heads, or limping on broken legs, meet us as we enter the thicket. Presently they increase to hundreds, all hastening—not with lamentations, thank God! but in silence to the rear. Uncertainty is almost worse than death. Oh! to get through this dark, this gloomy thicket!

"Drive on ! Hurry up !" comes from the Captain.

The few minutes in passing this thicket will never be forgotten. Our infantry, who had charged a heavy battery, had been torn to pieces. They came in troops from the field of slaughter, bleeding and dying. "Hurry up ! Let us help them !" said every brave heart. "Forward! Forward! Forward! Let us go to the open field." Oh, now we see the light in our front! Soon we will be on fighting ground, and then we will let them have it!

Sixteen guns wheel into line in a twinkling, and we are pouring a deadly fire into a battery on an opposite hill, which had made such havoc among our infantry—the yeomanry of the army, God bless them! See! these yeomen are now in good order, emerging from the woods on our right, and are flanking the battery at which we are firing, and the day is ours!

"Fire! Fire! Fire!" rang out from every sergeant of piece, as gun after gun belched forth its blazing, burning shells. The incessant roar deafens the cannoneers, and the battalion is enveloped in smoke. Just as the order was given to "cease firing," and while the smoke was clearing up in our front, a dark form was seen a few yards in front of the guns, moving towards us. The first impression was that, under cover of the hill, the enemy was charging us, and this was the leader of the charge, and the order was on the lip, "Fire!" But a second look satisfied us that this was some frightened man who had become bewildered, like a startled bird, and was unconsciously about to rush into a blazing furnace.

Our infantry are now on the opposite hill, and we rest joyously from our labor.

General Alexander is responsible for the following incident: "On Sunday morning, the 3rd of May, a section of the Parker Battery was in the Plank road, firing down it towards Chancellor's house. Several Yankee batteries were enfilading the road with their

fire, and it was a decidedly hot place. I was standing talking with Captain Parker when there came
by a private of infantry with two Yankee prisoners.
He was walking between the prisoners, with his gun
on his shoulder, when a percussion shell came tear-
ing along, and, cutting off the Confederate's leg just
at the knee, it struck the road a few feet further on,
and exploded, with a tremendous flying of dirt and
whizzing of fragments. The leg was cut off com-
pletely and carried away, and the poor fellow, drop-
ping his gun and falling backward on his hands, held
up the bloody stump and shouted out, 'Pick me up!
Pick me up! Why don't you pick me up?'—As if
he were a nine-pin, and would be all right if he
could only be set up again! Meanwhile the Yankee
prisoners rapidly took in the idea that the Plank
road was very unhealthy as a promenade, and they
broke for the shelter of the woods on either side.
As they did so, a little powder-monkey of Parker's
Battery ["Doc" Howard], running up from the
caissons with a cartridge, was convulsed with the idea
of the Yankee shells scaring the Yankees themselves,
and yelled out after them, 'What in h—ll are you
running from your own shells for?' It all took
place in a second almost, and in its mingling of the
comic and the tragic illustrated the hardening effects
of the war as much as anything I ever saw."

This gay "powder-monkey" was soon thereafter
severely wounded himself.

On our left was a fence, and beyond it a large
oak tree, under which some of the boys discovered

about four hundred new knapsacks, well filled with exactly what we wanted—new clothes—besides numberless other things. The "plunder" was immense and valuable. Among other things the Captain got seventy new oil-cloths—one for each man in his command—and, catching a stray horse of the enemy, loaded him at once with them, and sent him to the rear.

The best way for a soldier to carry clothing is on his back, and some of the officers and men in a giffy had doffed their old clothes and appeared in nice new linen, greatly to their comfort as well as appearance. Our section had scarcely finished this pleasant occupation before the order "Limber to the front" was heard. We pass ambulances and broken gun-carriages, and one beautiful three-inch rifle-piece that every battery commander longed to own. The enemy had made a last stand at Chancellorsville, and we now see the house on fire. They abandon the place, and the day is ours.

Of the section under Captain Parker there were six or seven men wounded, but none mortally.

Of all the cheerful, plucky fellows who fought under Parker, in this battle and many others, none was more deservedly loved and admired than Ned Moore. He was one of those ardent and devoted Southerners who came from beyond the Potomac, and stood up for Southern rights at the expense of sundered social ties and wrecked estates. He was always true to duty, but in this battle he was conspicuously gallant. He survived the war; but died

not many years thereafter, while yet in the youth of
a noble manhood.

" He liveth long who liveth well ;
   All else is life but flung away.
He liveth longest who can tell
   Of true deeds, truly done, each day."

CHAPTER VIII.

GETTYSBURG.

"I rode to the extreme front, where there were four pieces of rifled cannon, almost without any infantry support. To the non-withdrawal of these guns is to be attributed the otherwise surprising inactivity of the enemy." — COL. FREEMANTLE (of the British Army).

IN June, 1863, Lee's army began the grand movement which culminated in the battle of Gettysburg. By long and rapid marching our battalion soon passed over the Blue Ridge, and at sunset one warm, clear day we crossed the Shenandoah, and encamped near the pleasant village of Millwood. Here we rested awhile. Our tents were pitched under the ample shade of the trees on the grounds of a gentleman named Burwell. His residence was one of the handsomest in the Valley, and the grounds were of rare beauty.

There was a spring on this place which was remarkable even in that land of abundant and healthful waters. It flowed from under huge gray rocks, cold and sparkling, in a torrent that might have turned a mill-wheel. How we drank, and drank again, after our toilsome tramp over the mountains! How pleasantly we lolled on the grass, talking and laughing, little thinking that for some of us it was the last trysting-place on Virginia soil!

At Millwood we had an accession of two men who were destined to play a noble part in the history of the company—Gibson Clarke and Michael Spence.

I may not write of the great march into Pennsylvania; how it was boasted from man to man that our army was never in so good condition; how proudly we stepped upon Pennsylvania soil, determined to requite that great State and the whole North for the insults and injuries they had heaped upon our mother Virginia. This I will pass over, and introduce the reader at once into the stirring scenes of Gettysburg, where, I claim, the Parker Battery played a part conspicuously brilliant, and one which deserves to be recorded in the annals of the great war between the States.

With the First corps, under Longstreet, it was not our fortune to reach the battlefield until the afternoon of Thursday, the 2d of July, when was made our first advance, amidst circumstances that were indeed grand and thrilling.

On the slope of a wooded hill our infantry were forming for a charge. Federal infantry were thick in front of them, assisted by artillery, which poured a storm of shrapnel into our ranks. Rhett's battery, of our battalion, was already blazing away from the crest of the hill, and they were said to have lost thirty men in as many minutes; but we were as yet at its base.

"Cannoneers, mount! Forward!"

Quickly we rushed between the already moving

cannon-wheels, and nimbly sprang into our seats,—
all except John Hightower, who missed his hold,
and the great, heavy weight rolled over his body.
Did we halt? No! Not if your brother falls by
your side must you heed his dying wail! This is
the grim discipline of war.

Never shall I forget the scene presented on this
hill, which was about opposite the since famous
Round-Top mountain. The Federal shrapnel rattled
like hail through the trees around us, while our infantry, which was preparing to charge, swayed backward and forward, in and out, like a storm-cloud
vexed by contrary winds. There is an awful pause.
One of our men trembles and cowers. Like lightning Parker's sword circles the coward's head, and
he learns that there is danger in rear as well as in
front!

"Give it to them, boys!" said one of the infantry.

"We'll do it!" I responded.

"Ah, I see you are of the right grit," said he.

This compliment he paid me, I imagine, because
I smiled in his face in my answer, marching close up
to the muzzle of my piece. When he spoke to me
I was repeating the lines—

> " For right is right, since God is God,
>   And right the day must win ;
>   To doubt, would be disloyalty ;
>   To falter, would be sin ! "

Like many other conceited little beings who in-
habit this conceited little world, I had presumed to

interpret the will of GOD and anticipate His policy in the government of the world! How helpless a thing is the individual man! The winds of passion are blowing, and I am but a bubble on the crest of a storm-wave of war!

Fire! Fire! Fire! And each gun is discharging its leaden terrors into the ranks of the foe! But now comes the brave infantry. Wofford, of Georgia, his hat off and his bald head shining in the sun, dashes through our battery, followed by his brigade. Out flashed Captain Parker's sword, while the words "Hurrah for you of the bald head!" issued instantly from his lips. "Hurrah for you of the bald head!" was repeated by the cannoneers, while the charging Georgians swept down the hill-side, driving the retreating foe to the protection of the opposite hill.

Away we gallop down a contiguous road, and take an advanced position. Still the word is ever "Fire! Fire!" until the sun sets upon the field of strife.

As the shadows of coming night are falling around us, the flames leap out from our guns in lovely contrast. "Oh! Captain, this is beautiful!" said one of our sentimental soldiers.

In front of our guns were a number of Federal dead and wounded. That night several of us went to see about them. The wounded begged piteously for water. We had but little in our canteens, and could only partially satisfy the cravings of these unfortunate petitioners. One poor fellow, a Pennsylvanian, and mortally wounded, conversed with me, as I bent low to catch his words:

"Why did you all come over here?" he asked.

"We have come," I replied, "to give your people a taste of what we have had to suffer."

I did not speak in a harsh tone, though I think now my words were too hard for the ears of a dying man.

"Why is it," he continued, "that you always whip us? Every battle which I have been in we have been defeated."

The dying soldier then told me his name and residence, and sent messages to his relatives, supposing that our army would possess his home. I then left him, and, wrapped in my blanket near the guns, was soon asleep.

But what of the dying boy in blue? He probably went to his "long home" that night. How could I leave him thus to die alone? We had perhaps sung the same hymns in Sunday-school, and each had bent the knee before the same "Our Father." How could I leave him there on the hill-side, with no mother to kiss him—no sister to pray? Could I not watch with him just one hour—his last hour of mortal anguish? Did only the cold stars see him die? Heard only the night-winds his dying sigh? And he my brother, for whom Christ died! O Moloch of war, I hate you! O Philosophy of greed and glory, I abhor you! Tear down the monuments to the heroes of blood and gloom, and let the apostles of faith and hope and love stand bright and strong and beautiful—in sculpture, in painting, and in poetry— as typical of the redeemed and regenerated earth.

There was a man in our company who went down that night among the dead and wounded to plunder them. The next day he was killed. There was another man (Pat. McNeil) who, during the heavy cannonading previous to Pickett's charge, at the risk of his life, removed to a place of safety a wounded Federal lying in front of our guns. He had just returned from this errand of mercy when a cannon-shot tore off both his legs. He exclaimed, " Oh, my poor wife and children ! " and died.

Woolfolk's battery during the afternoon took position near a farm-house, and one of the men went into the house and found his own father and mother crouching in the cellar. He removed them to the rear as soon as practicable.

Parker fired the first cannon-shot at $4\frac{1}{4}$ A. M. on the great day of the Gettysburg battle,—the third day of July, 1863,—and, as it will be proven, he fired the last.

All the morning of that long and bloody day was occupied by the infantry in getting ready for the great struggle in the afternoon; but the artillery was kept busy. We were instructed to be sparing in the use of ammunition; but the Federal artillery evidently had plenty of it, for they pelted us almost incessantly, whether we held our peace or not. It was during this kind of fighting that we had two men killed—Loughridge and McNeil—and several wounded.

At one time Lieut. Brown ordered the men at

Sergeant William Cogbill's gun to retire a few paces from the piece and lie down. The air was hideous with Yankee missiles. One of the men said to his comrade, "Oh, I had much rather be at the gun!" The words had scarcely escaped his lips when a shot struck and shattered the wheel where he had been standing. The cannoneers at once sprang to the gun, quickly supplied it with a new wheel (carried for such contingencies), and resumed firing.

It was noticed that the aim of the enemy was not so accurate when we were allowed to return his salutes. Besides, it was a terrible strain to the nerves to lie down under such a fiery storm, and think!

There were several "conversions" (temporary) among the "Cockade Invincibles" about this time.

Presently a barn near by, where a number of Federal wounded had been put the night previous, was discovered to be on fire. The enemy's shells had ignited this building in which their own wounded lay. Andrew Barker, always kind and impulsive, raised the cry, "The wounded! The wounded!" Captain Parker ordered the battery to cease firing, and our boys and others of the battalion at once went to the rescue of these unfortunates, though it is feared some of them were burnt to death.

I was impressed by the coolness of a new recruit— Gibson Clarke. This was his first battle, and his demeanor was worthy of a veteran. His face reminded me of pictures I had seen of Napoleon, and I ever afterwards called him "Little Nap."

In the afternoon I saw General Alexander (who

in this battle had command of all Longstreet's artillery) ride up to our battery, and heard him say—

"Captain Parker, arrange your pieces *en eschelon*. The signal gun will be fired from the right. Take it up, and pass it to the left."

Seventy-five pieces of artillery, at this signal, commenced to roar in Longstreet's corps alone. Other guns in the corps of Ewell and Hill joined in the thundering concert. The enemy replied with equal or greater force. This was kept up until our artillery had lost many men and horses, and nearly exhausted their supply of ammunition, and then there was a strangely long pause.

And then stepped forth that "brave and gallant few," under George Pickett, who stormed and TOOK the heights of Gettysburg, but in the moment of victory were overwhelmed by sheer numbers. If Albion has the right to be proud of the six hundred who rode so grandly at Balaklava, surely Virginia need not be ashamed of her sons who walked so calmly through the fiery storm of that summer afternoon—calmly to wounds and death!

In the great cannonade preceding this charge our artillery suffered heavily. Owing to this, and the failure of ordnance supplies, after the repulse of Pickett, most of it was ordered to fall back. Only Parker's guns remained (at least that we saw) of all the seventy-five that had made such a brave show.

Presently one of our guns was sent to the rear, and the gun of Sergeant William Cogbill (who was wounded, but stuck to his post) was removed a few yards, so as to command a road up which the enemy's skirmishers were now advancing. When I saw that we were thus left almost alone, I went up to Lieut. Brown and said, " Captain Parker will let us all get cut to pieces."

" Don't say that," replied Brown, sternly. "Don't say that ! "

To speak discouragingly in battle is a grave military offence. I "stood corrected," and went to my gun.

Here I will introduce an extract from article on "Gettysburg and the Pennsylvania Campaign, which, appeared in the September (1863) No. of *Blackwood's* (Edinburgh) *Magazine*, from the pen of an English officer. This officer was Colonel Freemantle, who was present with the Confederate army as war correspondent:

"If Longstreet's conduct was admirable, that of General Lee was perfectly sublime. He was engaged in rallying and in encouraging the broken troops, and was riding about a little in front of the wood quite alone, the whole of his staff being engaged in a similar manner further to the rear. His face, which is always placid and cheerful, did not show signs of the slightest disappointment, care, or annoyance; and he was addressing to every soldier he met a few words of encouragement, such as, ' All this will come right in the end; we'll talk it over afterwards; but, in the meantime, all good men must rally. We want all good and true men just now,' etc. He spoke to all the wounded men that

10

passed him, and the slightly wounded he exhorted
to 'bind up their hurts and take up a musket.'
Very few failed to answer his appeal, and I saw
many badly wounded men take off their hats and
cheer him. . . . . . . He said to me, 'This has been a
sad day for us, Colonel—a sad day; but we can't
expect always to gain victories.' He was also kind
enough to advise me to get into a more sheltered
position.

"Notwithstanding the misfortune which had so
suddenly befallen him, General Lee seemed to observe
everything, however trivial. When a mounted officer began licking his horse for shying at the bursting of a shell, he called out, 'Don't whip him, Captain; don't whip him. I've got just such another
foolish horse myself, and whipping does no good.'*

"I saw General Willcox come up to him and explain, almost crying, the state of his brigade. Gen.
Lee immediately shook hands with him, and said
cheerfully : 'Never mind, General, all this has been
my fault; it is I that have lost this fight, and you
must help me out of it in the best way you can.'

---

* General Lee was talking with General Alexander when Col.
Freemantle came up. The "mounted officer," who "licked"
his horse, was F. M. Colston, General Alexander's chief of ordnance. Alexander had ordered Colston to go somewhere on an
errand, and his horse balked, not wanting to separate from Alex
ander's horse, as they generally rode together on the march. It
was this, and not the shell, that caused the "shying." Colston
was a youth of scarcely twenty, a Marylander, and gallant almost
to a fault. He was volunteer adjutant at Chancellorsville and
Gettysburg, and at this latter place his horse's bridle-rein was
cut by a bullet.

"It is difficult to exaggerate the critical state of affairs as they appeared about this time. If the enemy or their General had shown any enterprise, there is no saying what might have happened. General Lee and his officers were evidently impressed with a sense of the situation. . . . We heard that Generals Garnett and Armistead were killed, and General Kemper mortally wounded; also, that Pickett's division had only one field-officer unhurt. Nearly all this slaughter took place in an open space about one mile square, and within one hour.

"At six P. M. we heard a long and continuous Yankee cheer, which we at first imagined was an indication of an advance; but it turned out to be their reception of a general officer, whom we saw riding down the line, followed by about thirty horsemen.

"Soon afterwards I rode to the extreme front, where there were four pieces of rifled cannon almost without any infantry support. To THE NON-WITHDRAWAL OF THESE GUNS IS TO BE ATTRIBUTED THE OTHERWISE SURPRISING INACTIVITY OF THE ENEMY.

"I was immediately surrounded by a sergeant and about half a dozen gunners, who seemed in excellent spirits and full of confidence, in spite of their exposed situation. The sergeant expressed his ardent hope that the Yankees might have spirit enough to advance and receive the dose he had in readiness for them. . . . . . Whilst we were talking, the enemy's skirmishers began to advance slowly,

and several ominous sounds in quick succession told
us that we were attracting their attention, and that
it was necessary to break up the conclave. I therefore turned round and took leave of those cheery
and plucky gunners."

The "four pieces of rifled cannon" to which this
British critic alludes were undoubtedly two of
Parker's guns (two having been sent to the rear)
and two guns of the First Company of Richmond
Howitzers, under Lieutenant R. M. Anderson and
Sergeant J. V. L. McCreery. These were the only
guns then at the front.

It was now perhaps seven o'clock in the evening,
and we were still contesting the ground against the
Federal skirmishers, who kept up a continuous fire.
The two Howitzer guns had now retired, and only
one of ours was firing, as ammunition was nearly
exhausted. Lieutenant Brown noticed a cartridge
smoking as No. 2 inserted it into this gun, and ordered the detachment to cease firing and empty the
sponge bucket of water into it, to prevent premature
explosion. Captain Parker, noticing the cessation
of firing, came in great haste to know the cause.
When the lieutenant informed him he ridiculed the
idea, at the same time clapping his hands on the
gun. In an instant both hands were dangling above
his head in the air, and he vociferously exclaiming,
"Cool her off! Cool her off!" And *he* cooled off.

Captain Parker, appreciating the importance of
holding this position until nightfall, left us for a
few minutes to rally to our support some demoral-

ized infantry who were cowering behind the trees and rocks in the woods to the right of the road. There were only a few of them, scattered here and there, without much show of discipline. Realizing his exposed position, he sent a messenger to General McLaws to know why he was left there. General McLaws replied that it was an omission, and to withdraw.

Lieutenant Brown had fired all except three rounds of canister, which he held for the expected infantry charge.

Just then General Longstreet rode up and angrily inquired of Lieutenant Brown:

" Why are these guns here, sir ?   I thought I had ordered all the artillery from the field ? "

" We are here by Captain Parker's orders, General," replied Brown.

" Where is Captain Parker ? "

" I think he will be here in a moment, sir," answered the lieutenant.

In a little while Captain Parker returned.

" Why have you retained these guns here, Captain ? " demanded Longstreet.

" I have received no authentic orders to leave, General.   Besides, the position seemed to me to be important, and I thought I would hold it as long as possible."

Longstreet seemed now to be of the same opinion, for he told Parker if he could hold the position for a short while longer he would send him an infantry support.   In conversation afterwards with Colonel

Freemantle, General Longstreet said he thought "the enemy would have attacked had the guns been withdrawn."

With the infantry that soon came, we held back the Federal skirmishers, who were creeping up under cover of trees. We expected every moment that all the Federal artillery in our front would concentrate upon us; but, to our surprise, they did not, and allowed these two Richmond guns to keep back their infantry until nearly dark, when we quietly withdrew, and rejoined our disappointed comrades in the rear.

The Parker Battery had fired 1,142 rounds that day—the largest number during the war.

The loss in the Parker Battery was small, considering the character and length of the engagement. Killed: Joshua C. Hallowell, James B. Loughridge, and Pat. McNeil. Wounded: William B. Cogbill, Edward D. Moore, Sam. P. Weisiger, John Pearce, John A. Hightower, Thomas Forsett, John R. Baptist, Thomas J. Todd, George W. Hancock, and G. W. Madison.

The next day we buried Loughridge and McNeil on the field. The writer recollects cutting their names in a pine board, which was stuck at the head of the one grave. The body of Hallowell (who died at Williamsport) was brought to Virginia, and is interred in Hollywood cemetery.

The casualties in the battalion were heavy. Captain Moody had to borrow men from Barksdale's brigade to help work his howitzers.

From "the diary of an English officer," before quoted, are the following extracts:

"*July* 4.—At one P. M. the rain began to descend in torrents. General Longstreet talked to me for a long time about the battle. He said the mistake they had made was in not concentrating the army more, and making the attack with thirty thousand men, instead of fifteen thousand.

"*July* 5 (*Sunday*).—The night was very bad; thunder and lightning, torrents of rain; the road knee-deep in mud and water."

The retreat from Gettysburg was made in the midst of this bad weather. The most brotherly feeling existed among officers and men. I believe I rode Captain Parker's horse almost as much as he did. Other officers were similarly kind to cannoneers. Suffering bound us closer together.

Our little Corporal Howard met with a funny accident as we were marching at night. Coming to a stream across the road, he saw what appeared to be the other bank, and leaped towards it, only to find himself up to his chin in water! Wet clothes, however, were the "latest agony" in soldier fashions, and the mud was intolerable.

One of the men said on this retreat, "If I could end the war by raising my little finger, I wouldn't do it." George Goff said he ought to be killed; but the man meant only to express strongly his faith in overruling Providence. Near Hagerstown, where we halted for a while, he led the company prayer-meeting at night, and read from the Sixth chapter of the "Revelation of St. John." In glowing imagery the inspired seer there describes what followed the opening of the "sixth seal" by the appointed angel: how "there was a great earthquake, and the sun became black as sackcloth of hair, and the moon became as blood, and the stars of heaven fell unto the earth, even as a fig tree casteth her untimely figs when she is shaken of a mighty wind:" how "the heaven departed as a scroll when it is rolled together," and "the great day of wrath had come." Was there not some appropriateness in this selection just after the mighty tempest at Gettysburg?

Near Hagerstown the Confederates threw up breastworks, and awaited the attack of the victorious General Meade; but we were discreetly let alone. I never saw our men more eager for a fight. They seemed anxious for a chance to atone for the failure at Gettysburg.

We cross the Potomac unmolested, and continue our march towards the Blue Ridge and beyond. Reaching the Shenandoah, we find that river turbid and swollen by the recent rains, and more suggestive of "the swelling of the Jordan" than of the limpid beauty which led the Indians to call it "the daughter of the stars."

The current is strong, and I am slenderly made, and, resisting all I can, it is pushing me off my feet, and bearing me down stream. Dear, genial, sturdy Pat Brooks catches me in his arms, and leads me safely across.

Dear Pat, if I had all the gold and all the glory

of this transitory world to give thee, they would be the merest baubles compared with the gift thou mayest have, and which I most cordially wish thee. And it is this: That when thou art called to cross the mystic Jordan, an Arm of everlasting strength may encircle thee, and bear thee safely to the everlasting shore!

But, oh! the mountains that rise, dark and strong, against the orient sky! Must we climb those rugged heights? Faith whispers, Be strong; and Hope, on tiptoe, beckons to the GLORY BEYOND!

CHAPTER IX.

THE TENNESSEE CAMPAIGN.

"Ah! who may tell of the suffering cast
O'er North and South in that gory past!
Or reckon the hosts that met in the fray,
Who sighed on those fields their life away?
Or the bright day-dreams of the fallen brave
That sank with their bones in the dreamless grave?
Or number the hearths where widows sit,
With their fatherless ones, disconsolate?"
— *Whittet, ("The Brighter Side of Suffering.")*

WHEN, in September, 1863, General Longstreet, with the divisions of Hood and McLaws, went to northern Georgia, he took with him only one battalion of artillery, and that was Alexander's—a compliment which the command did not fail to appreciate.

Passing by rail through the Carolinas and part of Georgia, we were the recipients of honors and hospitalities that reminded us of the enthusiasm that marked the first year of the war. At Sumter, in South Carolina, the people gave us food, and at Aiken the ladies stood on a bridge over the railroad and showered flowers upon the soldiers as the cars passed underneath. At Augusta, in Georgia, we were hospitably entertained, and on the way between that city and Atlanta ladies of the best society came to the depots and waved their handkerchiefs in our honor.

From Atlanta we hastened to Dalton, and from thence to the scene of the great struggle on the banks of the Chicamauga—a tortuous stream, and, true to its Indian derivation, a "stream of death" to many sons of the battling North and South. We arrived too late, however, to participate in this fight; but under the direction of our Doctor-Captain we rendered some assistance to the wounded. The weather (September) was hot and very dry, and the condition of the wounded was pitiable beyond description. In many cases the best that we could do was to cut bushes and fasten them in the ground so to shade these poor sufferers from the glare of the sun.

While encamped in this section the battery received an accession in the person of that genial gentleman, Thomas L. Alfriend, who was made orderly sergeant, and so continued to the close of the war.

The battalion was soon ordered forward in the direction of Chattanooga, where the enemy awaited us. How frequently we crossed the Chicamauga on that march! The crooked stream seemed to dispute our advance every half hour!

Arriving in front of Chattanooga, we halted behind Missionary Ridge. Here the drought was followed by excessive rains, so that, together with insufficient clothing and food, some of our boys got sick, and had to be sent back to the hospitals at Rome, and other places in Georgia. Among the sick boys was David C. Richardson, who had but lately recovered from a wound received at Manassas.

When the frequent rains at last retreated before the orient beams of a clear day, we saw Lookout Mountain, tall and lonely, standing as a sentinel among the hills. Before many days the Parker battery, having light three-inch rifled pieces, was ordered to ascend it, and from thence to shell the enemy.

On one side Lookout Mountain rises almost precipitously to a height of fifteen hundred feet, its base being washed by the Tennessee river. The ascent, even by the regular road, was difficult; and the command, "Cannoneers to the wheels!" was frequently given—the men having to assist the horses in their arduous task. As we toiled up the steep road glimpses of scenery of surpassing beauty were afforded here and there. Picturesque valleys suddenly opened far below, while beetling rocks above seemed ready to topple on us. Add to the emotions naturally produced by such scenes the fact that we were marching to fight a brave and skilful enemy, who might fire on us at any moment from an opposite elevation, and you can imagine that the boys were very much interested!

A halt was ordered on a plateau, when we were as yet far below the top of the mountain. Opposite, and within easy range, was a Federal battery, which we called the "Moccasin," from the resemblance of the hill it occupied to a shoe. The "Yanks" were well entrenched there, and had been troubling our infantry with too many salutes. The Parker guns now opened on the "Moccasin" battery, and pretty soon convinced it that it had better let our infantry alone.

The next morning the ascent of the mountain was resumed. Our eyes were feasted with sights of the grand and beautiful as we toiled upward, but these scarcely prepared us for the glory of the view from the summit. It seemed almost limitless. In front, to the right, to the left, mountain on mountain loomed tall and blue, as far as vision might extend, while the Tennessee river, winding gracefully among them, gleamed out here and there in bright relief. Mountains that kissed the skies of the distant Carolinas might be seen, as well as those of nearer Georgia and Alabama; while far, far north—can it be so, or does my eager heart deceive me?—dear old Virginia and her daughter Kentucky hold up holy hands in adoring reverence from the footstool of the great Creator.

The view gave me a better idea of the infinite than I had ever hoped to obtain, and for the moment almost overwhelmed me with emotion. The camps of both grand armies were seen at a glance.

There is a jutting rock, facing Chattanooga, on which I have often stood as a sentinel during the witching hours of the night. It juts from the mountain-side several yards. From thence every fire in the Federal army might be seen, while the outer line, like a flaming crescent, marked its limits. Then an intervening dark space, and the opposite Confederate fires glared against the sky.

An ex-Federal officer visited this rock since the

war, escorting some ladies. He was, it seems, under the influence of liquor, and, wishing to be brave in the presence of the fair, he ventured too near the edge, and toppled over, to be dashed to pieces on the rocks or tree-tops far below!

What weird thoughts coursed through my brain during some of those sentinel hours on that jutting rock! Away down in the valleys it might be calm, but there, almost every night, the winds would rise, and seemed not voiceless in their unrest. The trees swayed to and fro, and rustled their leaves; but it was not simply sound—there was sympathy expressed: "Poor, insane humanity," seemed saying the moaning winds, "poor, warring humanity! Look to the everlasting hills for your help—even above thee—for the Right and the True!" The sharp report of a picket gun startles the valley below; the winds moan drearily; the clouds descend upon the mountain, and cling to the trees, weeping that the voice is not heard.

The "Moccasin" battery returned the first shots that we fired from our lofty position, and one shell narrowly missed General Bragg, who was with us at the time; but they did not seem to know that they could reach us, and seldom or never replied to us afterwards. Every morning, about nine o'clock, our business-like firing commenced, and was generally kept up in leisurely style until night.

Late one chilly evening, in the latter part of October, General Longstreet visited the mountain and took coffee with Captain Parker. It was

whispered among us that something important was
about to happen; and at last it passed from lip to
lip that an attack was to be made that night by
General Jenkins on a "Yankee" wagon train, on
the road to Chattanooga, and supposed to be thinly
guarded. The wind was so high that it was with
difficulty we kept our fires from being blown away.
Wrapped in our thin blankets, we went to sleep,
thinking about the "night attack." Not long after
midnight we were awakened by the booming of a
single cannon in the valley below. The attack had
begun. Running to the jutting rocks on the mountain we beheld a scene that for weird grandeur and
tragic interest will not soon be forgotten. The battle was before us as a picture: the rapidly advancing Confederates, told by the flash of their muskets
and the peculiar yell, and the blaze of a single Federal cannon, with the accompanying flashes of their
infantry. The enemy were quickly and strongly reinforced, and Jenkins and his South Carolinians were
driven back before they had time to eat much supper.
The conduct of our "Northern brethren" was at
least unscriptural: the Palmetto boys had gone for
bread, and they gave them bullets!

Lookout Mountain was a summer resort, and on
it were a number of cottages for visitors, and a
chapel. The holy Sabbath came with its calming
influence to us, as to all who love it, and some of us
went into the chapel. I recollect that we failed to
get rations that morning, and were quite hungry;
but I did not know what angels' food awaited me.

We had heard something about the reverend old
man who was going to preach.   Forty years before,
it was said, he had told the story of the Cross to the
Indians on this very mountain.   I do not remember
his sermon, or any portion of it; but he read and
sang a hymn that has been ringing in my heart ever
since.   It was Watts' sublime paraphrase of the
Ninetieth Psalm—"the prayer of Moses, the man
of God":

> O God, our help in ages past,
> Our hope for years to come!
> Our shelter from the stormy blast,
> And our eternal home!
>
> Before the hills in order stood,
> Or earth received her frame,
> From everlasting Thou art God!
> To endless years the same!
>
> Under the shadow of Thy throne
> Still may we dwell secure:
> *Sufficient is Thine arm alone,*
> And our defence is sure.

The reverend man read these words slowly and
solemnly, and then sang them to a tune which
seemed peculiarly suited to their deep, divine mean-
ing,—a few of us joining with him.   Then, if never
before, I felt that I worshipped GOD.   The petty
cares and dangers of my individual life, and even
the concerns of warring nations, dwindled into insig-
ficance before the Supreme Eternal, whose infinite
power and immutable love were emblemed so glori-
ously by the "everlasting hills" around me.   On

the toilsome march and the contested field, in after days, these pure words cheered me; and in the yet more significant and dangerous conflicts of civil life —in battles with the mean and the wicked, within and without, and in all the weariness of our swift-passing vanities—an influence has followed me from those holy words, turning my vascillating heart towards the Ineffable Good—the ETERNAL GOD.

During our stay before Chattanooga, President Davis made a visit to General Bragg's army. It was rumored in camp that a council of war was held, and the plan of a grand campaign adopted. Just about that time a conversation is said to have been held between one of Bragg's pickets and an opposite blue-coat, which, had we only suspected it, was indicative, and even prophetic, of said plan and its results. Said the Federal (alluding to our victory of Chicamauga): "I say, Johnny, you beat us that time, but as soon as Longstreet goes away we'll give you the d—d'st whipping you ever had in your life!"

On or about the 10th of November, 1863, the battalion received marching orders. The order came at night, and as quietly as possible the horses were harnessed, and the command moved silently down the mountain.

At the beginning of this campaign the battery was officered as follows: W. W. Parker, captain; J. Thompson Brown, Jordan C. Parkinson, George E. Saville, lieutenants; Thomas L. Alfriend, Wm. B. Cogbill, John A. Cogbill, James M. Tyler, Matt.

11

Condrey, sergeants; J. W. Verlander, David C. Richardson, James E. Darden, Philip V. Scherer, George W. Jones, John W. Moody, R. E. Dunaway, Gibson Clarke, corporals.

The command proceeded by rail to Sweetwater, a pleasant village on the East Tennessee and Georgia railroad, where we encamped for several days. We then crossed the river at Loudon, the Federal troops retreating before us. The enemy's force was evidently small, and intended only to retard our advance on Knoxville. An effort was soon made by General Longstreet to compel this force to fight, and he, perhaps, hoped to capture the whole of it. The result was an engagement near Campbell Station, mainly of artillery. It commenced about two o'clock in the afternoon, and lasted until night.

As our infantry advanced a hare was scared up and scampered away, occasioning the expression of a sentiment from one of the men that was pretty general at the time: "Go it, old hare," said the facetious warrior, "I'd run too if I didn't have a reputation to sustain!"

As it was the first time we had met in fair open field fight with these Western soldiers, I recollect there was some little trepidation among the men at Billy Cogbill's gun as their first shots exploded over us. "Too much excitement at that gun!" sternly said Lieutenant Saville, and the boys applied themselves to work with their old-time steadiness.

Parker's guns occupied during the fight five different positions, advancing at each move. Towards

night we found ourselves considerably in advance of
our own infantry, and our Captain, believing that
he could go even still farther with comparative
safety, asked permission to do so. As the battery
dashed forward, General Longstreet lifted his hat in
compliment to our intrepid leader. Down the hill
and across a stream we galloped, some of us expecting every moment to receive a deadly volley from
the enemy; but, to our surprise, the Federals retreated before us without a shot, thinking us to be
strongly supported. Our own infantry, under Gen.
Kershaw, were in the woods on our right flank, and
finding us in the position where a " Yankee" battery
had been, they were about to charge us, but found
out their mistake in time.

Then commenced a well-directed fire from the
enemy's guns, which had gained another position,
resulting in the killing and wounding of several
men in a Georgia battery under Colonel Ledbetter.
Some of the Federal shots were singularly effective.
One shot, to instance, passed through two horses,
and then crushed both legs and an arm of a man
who was standing at the caisson. So destructive
was the enemy's fire that our men were driven from
their guns. For reasons not known to me, no other
battery was ordered to the support of the unfortunate Georgians, and their disabled gun was allowed
to remain where it was, the Federals still raking the
spot with well-directed shots. Captain Winthrop,
of Colonel Alexander's staff (and late of the Twenty-
second British infantry), went to the deserted piece

and shot one of the wounded horses to end its misery. The soldier who had had his legs and arm crushed begged Winthrop, in piteous tones, to shoot him also. Winthrop, however, hastened to our battery, and telling Dr. (Captain) Parker of the pitiable condition of the wounded man, asked for morphine to carry to him that his death might be made more easy.

"No," replied the Captain, "I will go."

"I insist upon going," replied the brave Winthrop. I am alone in the world; you have a wife. I will go."

"I am a doctor now," answered Captain Parker. And though the enemy's fire was still concentrated upon the dangerous position, he went to it and administered the opiate to the dying Georgian. Under its Lethean touch, soon visions of sweet home and of faces of kind friends hide from sight the dead horses and broken gun, to be followed, we trust, by visions of heaven and of faces "long gone before."

Night stopped the fighting, which had not proved very serious to either side; and the enemy, who was evidently anxious to gain the fortifications around Knoxville, stealthily continued his retreat. Our corps encamped that night in advance of the battlefield of the afternoon.

The next morning, while prowling around a farmhouse in search of a "bite" of breakfast, I heard a negro woman ask, "Ain't them-uns had no breakfast?" This shocked even my ear impolite almost as much as the fact that I was one of "them-uns."

Some war "poet" compiled these improved pronouns into verses. Thus:

> " 'Tis hard for you-uns to sleep in camp ;
>   'Tis hard for you-uns through rain to tramp ;
>   'Tis hard for you-uns and we-uns to part,
>   For you-uns has stolen we-uns's heart."

The Parker Battery was in the lead during the whole of this march. Light skirmishing was had each day, the enemy endeavoring to delay our advance as much as possible. Just before we reached Knoxville their artillery attempted to take position, but Parker was so quick in his movements that he drove them before him before they could fire a shot.

Arriving before the city, General Longstreet commenced preparations to assault and capture it. The brave Captain Winthrop was severely wounded in some preliminary skirmishing. In a ditch running obliquely with the road to the city about two hundred infantry were posted to dispute our advance. An attempt was made to dislodge them with some light guns, but in vain. Captain Taylor's "Napoleons" were then ordered to the work, and a few well-directed shots covered up some of the men in the ditch, and they began to get out and take to their heels. Just then an infantry company was ordered to charge the ditch. They had to make quite an ascent to reach it, and halted for a moment to gain breath. Captain Winthrop, thinking they lacked courage, spurred his horse forward and charged the enemy alone. A volley of oaths to "shoot down the d——d rebel," was quickly followed by a volley of bullets, and Winthrop was dismounted, with a fractured collar-bone. Though so dangerously wounded, he walked calmly up to Captain Parker (about two hundred yards away), and asked him to examine his wound. In the Maryland campaign this brave fellow charged a company of Yankee cavalry alone, and killed the first man he met.

Two of our best men, Sergeant Edward D. Moore and Leonidas R. Tucker, were captured about this time and held as prisoners until near the close of the war. The story of the hardships they endured would fill a book; but those were troublous times.

The Parker boys can hardly forget the "sick flour" that was issued as rations before Knoxville. How particularly nice the biscuits looked on that frosty morning! They were eagerly devoured, little heed being taken to a certain queer taste about them. Soon after breakfast, however, nearly everybody was sick—a dull, nauseating, continued sickness. What was the cause? It was discovered that the wheat had lobelia mixed with it, and our eight days' supply of flour was useless. There was no escape—we must either eat the sickening bread or none. Impelled by hunger, some of us tried it again, and with the same nauseating result. Thus, for over a week, and in the face of the enemy—alternately marching, fighting, and digging—we had to live as best we could without bread. Our substitute was corn, boiled or parched as opportunity afforded.

The morning of Sunday, November 29th, broke chilly and damp upon Longstreet's little army. The night previous the clouds hung low around the hills on which we were posted, and rain fell at intervals. Unusual movements seemed to indicate something important as impending. Light had scarcely broken through the murky east when these ominous signs were fulfilled. The attack on Knoxville had commenced. After a brave effort, the Confederates were repulsed ; and about noon there was a truce to allow us to bury our dead.

Major Frank Huger, of our battalion, was among those who went forward under the flag of truce. During the interview that ensued, one of the Federal officers asked our Major about what he called the "White-horse Battery," and said he had particularly noticed it at Campbell Station. This was our battery, which in the Tennessee campaign had an unusual number of white horses.

Never, perhaps, was I so deeply impressed with the wickedness of war as on that cloudy Sunday morning. Occasionally there was a lull in the firing, during which we lay near our guns ready to resume the hazardous work. It was during these intervals that my mind reverted to the nature of our employment. Waiving the questions that had brought the sections into armed conflict, it seemed to me so inherently wicked that God's intelligent creatures should thus destroy each other. There may be peo-

ple who will smile at this unsophisticated sentiment
who ought to weep: the unscrupulous orators, who
charmed and deceived the credulous multitudes;
the sordid devotees of Mammon, who bartered blood
for gold; the champions of honor, so called, who
made a sport of life and love and beauty, destroyed,
sorrowful, blasted; and even the ministers of holy
Heaven, who besieged the Supreme Arbiter with
their countercries, and pledged the loving God to
speak from the cannon's mouth.

The excitement of battle often produces intense
thirst. As soon as I knew of the truce, my first
thought was as to how to obtain water, having had
none at the guns. Our position was on a hill overlooking Knoxville, and below ran clear and cold the
waters of a river. True, the enemy was on the opposite bank and in close shooting range; but there
was peace, blessed peace, if but for a few hours.
How to get to the water puzzled us—George Jones
and me. The descent from the place where our
guns were posted was almost precipitous; so we repaired to another point, taking with us an old coffee-
pot, in which to bring back some of the precious
fluid. By holding on to trees and bushes we advanced about fifty yards, when the descent was
found so abrupt that I concluded to put down the
coffee-pot and reconnoitre. We had gone but a few
yards when down came the coffee-pot tumbling past
us, itself seemingly reconnoitering in a most lively
style, and we soon knew its fate by a significant
plash in the water below. We ventured a little

further down, when we were brought to a dead halt
by a yawning precipice, while just below the long-
desired stream flowed plentifully, but not for us.
We could now appreciate the fable of Tantalus and
the ever-deceiving waters. Thirsty before our ad-
venturous quest, and that thirst intensified by subsequent exertion, we could only stand upon a precipitous rock, and see, but not drink the cooling waters below.

Rumors were rife that a great battle had been
fought before Chattanooga, and General Bragg badly
defeated. Moreover, it was said that the victorious
enemy had sent a large force to attack Longstreet in
the rear. Orders to march soon came. Before
leaving our breastworks we cut logs from trees, and
burnt them so as to resemble as much as possible our
artillery pieces. Leaving these "Quaker guns" in
the breastworks to deceive the enemy as long as
possible, we, with the real guns, silently and at
night, commenced our mournful march, with our
faces towards Virginia. Our base of operations had
been North Georgia, and from that direction winter
clothing and shoes had been sent us. The disaster
at Chattanooga had necessitated the destruction of
these supplies while they were on the way. The
cold and snows of winter were upon us; all the
railroad bridges, and, in some cases, the tracks, had
been destroyed for a hundred miles in our rear; and
with only our summer clothing and badly shod, and
in some cases shoeless, we were about to enter upon
a career of hardships perhaps unequalled in the ex-

perience of any other corps during the entire four years of the great American war.

Now was needed that "sufficient Arm" about which we had heard and sung on Lookout mountain. In the forced night-march, through cold and rain, and with the gloomy prospect of war for years to come, that Arm, unseen, was near—and sufficient. Not in the tender embraces of home and loved ones could we be more surely protected and sustained. True, the path was rough, and timid nature sighed for peace and rest; but we were to be taught that the way to real excellence is through toil and danger, and, if need be, humiliation.

CHAPTER X.

THE TENNESSEE CAMPAIGN.

(*Continued.*)

"I might describe the barefooted men going home on furlough from East Tennessee. Tom Reed started through the snow with his feet tied up in rags, and when, after a tramp of many miles, he reached the cars at Bristol, they were bare and bleeding. A little girl, standing in a doorway, saw him and burst into tears, and gave him a pair of socks. . . . . When John Hawkins got to his father's dooryard the dogs barked at the ragged boy and kept him out until the servants called out, "It's Massa Johnny."— *Captain John Donnell Smith.*

THE people of East Tennessee were generally loyal to the United States government, in spite of the ordinance of secession passed by their State. "Lincoln coffee" and "Jeff. Davis coffee," as names for the real article or a substitute, in the common parlance of the people, indicated quite clearly their preference for the Union. It need scarcely be added that their loyalty was far more abundant than their "Lincoln" coffee.

"Men-folks" were conspicuously scarce, and women and "cotton-head" children remarkably numerous. Where were the men? Either in the Union army or hiding in the mountains. There were few comparatively in the Confederate army.

It was among these unfriendly people that Long-street's corps spent the winter of 1863–'4; and from them he had to obtain subsistence for man and beast. This was done by "impressing," which was but another name for legalized robbery. True, the owner of the forage or food impressed received pay (or a promise to pay) in Confederate scrip; but that was a sign of value which in 1864 was not much admired by true Confederates,—how much less by people who loathed the very name of President Davis!

If there were no men to fight or curse us when we went on these "impressing" expeditions, the women and children tried to substitute for their absent protectors. Even the children would stand on the fences, as we drove off with a wagon-load of hay, and shake their little fists and hurl epithets at us more forcible than elegant.

The tone of "society," as we saw it, is indicated by the following song, which was sung, with piano accompaniment, by a girl, in the hearing of several "Johnny Rebs":

I would not marry a Virginia boy,
I would not marry a Virginia boy,—
     They are so small,
     And they never grow tall,—
I would not marry a Virginia boy!

I would not marry a Georgia boy,
I would not marry a Georgia boy,—
     They are so yaller,
     They look like taller,—
I would not marry a Georgia boy!

I would not marry a South Car'lina boy,
I would not marry a South Car'lina boy,—
   They are such traitors,
   And they live on taters,—
I would not marry a South Car'lina boy !

I would not marry a Texas boy,
I would not marry a Texas boy,—
   They live on the level,
   And look like the devil,—
I would not marry a Texas boy !

I'm goin' to marry a Tennessee boy !
I'm goin' to marry a Tennessee boy !
   He wears the blue,
   And his heart is true !
I'm goin' to marry a Tennessee boy !

Captain John Donnell Smith writes of the Parker boys: "They were neatly uniformed, had the brisk look of city lads, and were noticeably young and of small stature. Their nice clothes were worn out before I again saw them; but the boyish look and spirit remained to the end as *differentiæ* of the company." It must have been their "small stature," and not their "nice clothes," that was noticed by our Tennessee songstress; and her auditors could not have been tall Tom Perdue and "old wheel-horse" Tom Evans, but some such Lilliputians as Carter Weisiger, or John S. Gary, or Andrew Barker.

Sam Weisiger, another Lilliputian, was condoling with a "Madison Tip" who was under punishment for some breach of discipline. "Moody," said Sam, speaking of the captain of the "Tips," "is a mean

man any way." "He's a much better man than
your Parker," quickly replied the Tip; "for he enlisted a lot of brats in the army, and draws rations
for them as men !"

Perhaps it may be well to give a list of soldier
garments for the season. It is scarcely long enough
to prove tedious: Jacket, pants, cotton shirt and
drawers, and anything in the place of shoes we could
pick up. Some of the men were barefooted, and
few had shoes that effectually protected their feet.
Overcoats were exceptional, and those were obtained
on the battlefields.

Did everybody get sick, "catch" colds or rheuma-
tism? No; we became as tough as Indians. That
winter I wrote to a lady in Richmond that nothing
but a bullet could kill me. The situation was similar
to that of an Irishman in a certain anecdote. He
was scouting early in the morning, intent on poach-
ing, in the park of a nobleman, when, to his surprise,
whom should he meet but the noble lord himself.
Embarrassed, but ready-witted, the Irishman quickly
said, "Good morning to your lordship ! And what
brings your lordship out so early this morning ? "
"Ah, Patrick," said the nobleman, languidly, " I'm
trying to get an appetite for my breakfast." "And
I," said Pat, "am trying to get a breakfast for my
appetite ! "

This reminds me of Pat Brooks, who left the
"Madison Tips" and joined the Parker boys—perhaps that his particular talent for "impressing"
might not have so much rivalry. Pat claimed to be

of Scotch nativity; and "Caledonia, stern and wild," would seem to be indeed a "meet nurse" for him; for a wild boy was Pat, and stern too, if need be. Pat always carried a rifle, but not to shoot Yankees. It was not usual for artillerymen to carry rifles, and it was generally believed among the men that Pat shot pigs and other domestic "game" with this weapon. It was said that one day he went into the yard of a farm-house, and, seeing a pig, he raised his rifle to shoot the "ferocious" brute, when the lady of the house rushed to the door, exclaiming, "Please, Mister, don't shoot my pig!" Pat, with a look of injured innocence and dignity, paused a minute, and then said, "Oh, be off with you now! You are just after making me lose my aim!" Though Pat was universally esteemed a good soldier, there were few who received a morsel from his well-filled and greasy haversack without some qualms of conscience.

The half-clad and always hungry "rebs," even the most law-abiding, availed themselves of any trivial excuse to enter the houses of the people. One excuse was, "I just want to get a light for my pipe." Once inside of the house, the cold and hungry soldier remained, however unwelcome a guest, until the hostess would be willing to feed him to get rid of him. If there happened to be anything cooking on the fire, the hungry visitor would seem almost to devour it with his eyes, and thus compel a reluctant invitation to dine.

A woman who lived on the road-side was cruelly

kind enough to save the marching soldiers the trouble of coming to the house for a light for their pipes. She posted one of her little sons at the gate with a pan full of live coals, and every smoker was invited to get a light there! When David Richardson came up to this boy, he quickly opened one of his pockets and said, "Pour it in!" "Why, it's fire!" said the boy. "Pour it in!" said Davy, in a louder tone. "Why, it's fire!" exclaimed the boy, his eyes big with astonishment. Just then his mother screamed out from the house, "Pour it in, Jamie! Pour it in! If I was there, I'd do it!" And she doubtless would—and down his throat, for that matter; for she evidently did not like the "Davis" men. Perhaps she mistook Richardson for that very scarce individual, a "fire-eater" in the army during the last years of the war!

Near Rogersville, in the earlier part of December, 1863, we halted in our march from Knoxville, and received three days half-rations. These rations were given us with instructions to be careful in their use, as a fight was expected. At the close of the first day my haversack was empty, and I wondered if I would ever again get enough bread to eat. On the 14th of December we encountered the enemy near Beans Station, and a spirited engagement ensued. Only two batteries of our battalion were engaged— Taylor's and Parker's.

As Lieutenant Brown was posting some guns near a farm-house, a woman came up and coolly requested him to "move them things out of her yard."

Tom Kirtley's leg was struck by a piece of shell, and his pocket-book thrown out on the ground. He said: "Well, I always thought the Yankees was mighty sharp fellows, but I didn't think they could pick a fellow's pocket a mile off!"

Sergeant Alfriend saw an Ohio newspaper, soon after this battle, in which a writer, after describing the preliminary skirmishing, said: "Presently two splendidly served rebel batteries ran into position, the shots from which told with terrible effect." The Federals were worsted and driven.

Among the results of this battle was the capture of a lot of coffee ("Lincoln") and sugar. These were distributed among us as a Christmas present. That night we slept on the field; but Tom Todd and I, before "retiring," went into a farm-house near by and "looked" at some corn-cakes on the fire until we were invited to eat some.

The following night we encamped near the Holston river. The weather was very cold; but we were well drilled to make the best of circumstances. After building a huge fire against the stump of a tree, and cooking and eating supper, the next thing to be considered was comfortable sleeping. No matter if it was for only one night, we would get straw if it could be obtained within a mile or two. This was spread on the ground, with a log of wood at the foot to keep it from being kicked into the fire. There were, I believe, seven or eight men in our mess; hence there were seven or eight blankets. Two of these were spread on the straw, and the

12

others used as covering. As these blankets lapped over each other, the covering was abundant, except possibly for the men on the outside or flanks. I assure you I never slept more comfortably in my life than I did on that cold, clear night, though in the morning there was frost in my hair!

Early that morning we crossed the Holston river on flat-boats. Ice was floating even in that rapid stream. The men had to pull the boats, loaded with guns and horses, by means of a rope stretched from shore to shore. Whilst we held one part of the rope the other fell into the water, so that it was soon encrusted with ice from end to end. Our hands were gloveless, and it was a test of fortitude to hold tightly to the rope and pull a loaded boat across the Holston. "Oh, we must let go!" pleaded the benumbed hands. "Obey orders!" curtly responded Duty. On one of these trips some one did unloose his grasp, and the boat drifted down the stream: but was recovered.

We had about two weeks rest and plenty to eat at Morristown, where we next stopped. Some of our boys gratefully remember Mr. Corse, who received them hospitably in his house; also Miss Dale, who gave one of them a new jacket. We laughed and grew fat at Morristown, with only one embarrassing incident that I recollect. Our mess, with "mother" Barker in charge, resided in a little house that was erected on blocks, and any small animal could get under it. It seems that goats had been using it as a place of shelter before our coming. The first night of our repose in this shanty we were awakened by a loud cry from Barker, "Goats! Goats!" and out he went, stick in hand, to drive the goats from under the house. The odor of this animal is never liked by any one, I believe; but it was unbearably offensive to the nostrils of Barker. No matter how cold the night and snugly he might be wrapped in his blanket, their presence would break his slumber, and with the cry of "Goats! Goats!" he would spring out of bed and drive them away.

We had been in quarters at Morristown about two weeks when we were again ordered to march. In fact, as the event proved, the Parker boys were selected from the battalion for active service the whole winter, while the main army lay quietly resting in our rear. With Generals Bushrod Johnson and Gracie's brigades we were kept to the front nearly the whole time, and frequently slept without tents.

Luckily, the winter was mild. For several weeks the weather was like "Indian summer." A smoky haze covered the mountains, and the sun shone red and warm at its setting. There was but little rain, and no snow, and the streams in this romantic mountain section ran beautifully clear. We crossed the French Broad river frequently in our marching and countermarching. When we were about to cross it the first time, I went up to Private D——, whom I knew to be very illiterate, and told him that the French Broad was so called because it divided the Confederacy from France, and that it was the purpose of General Longstreet to cross that river and

retreat into France! To which D—— replied, after
a moment's meditation, "I tell you, Mr. Cannon, I
aint goin' to no France! I'se got a wife and chillun
in this country, and I aint goin' to no France!"

One Sunday we crossed the French Broad three
times. It was not the place of the soldier to inquire
why these seemingly useless manœuvres were made.
The first, second, and last article in the good soldier's
creed is, Obedience.

To those who had eyes for the sublime and beautiful there was compensation in these long marches.
Perhaps no section of America is more abundant in
scenes of wild beauty than that through which the
French Broad breaks its way to join its sister rivers
that hasten to the Father of Waters. Pen and pencil combined, be they ever so eloquent or skilful,
would fail to picture the looming of the Alleghanies
against the eastern sky, as those mountains rise, like
a heaven-built wall, between North Carolina and
Tennessee; or the streams that press through these
natural barriers, and, in their rush and roar, make
music of the sweetest and wildest, and beauty of the
softest and grandest; or the solemn forests on the
hillsides, and the valleys laughing with tall corn;
and the voice of Nature through all, whispering an
ineffable something that pen never expressed and
pencil never portrayed.

Perhaps you may imagine that the war was an
unpropitious time to "muse on nature with a poet's
eye." Two years of life in the woods and fields,
however, had changed even the most delicate city

boys into hardened backwoodsmen. There were some among us, at least, who lost all taste for the artificial routine of civil life.

"The woods were God's first temples." See that youth, as he leaves the temporary camp, and walks alone into the woods. He is not of the "Cockade Invincible" or "Pat Brooks" style of soldier. He is one of "the prayer-meeting fellows." He is going to prayer-meeting now; but to meet Whom? It is winter, but the woods are beautiful. Besides the oak and chestnut and hickory, on whose bare limbs a few seared leaves dangle in the wind, there is the cedar, the spruce-pine, and other evergreens. The "prayer-meeting fellow" pauses near a snug thicket of these trees and bushes, and then moves on. He is looking for a "temple." He wishes to find a copse that will screen him from the eye of any possible traveller in this sylvan solitude. Presently he sees one that pleases even his critical eye, and, gently parting the interlacing branches, he finds himself in the place of prayer. On his knees, and with hands reverently clasped, he adores—what? The Beautiful? Surely this were a fitting spot for such æsthetic devotion. But, no: "O THOU that hearest prayer!" is the address on his lips. "The God of Israel"—the personal, all-pervading Spirit—is the awful being before whom he bends the knee, and whose blessing he supplicates, in the name of the holy Son of Mary. For mother, sisters, and brothers he prays, and loved ones near in spirit, but far away in body. For country and comrades he also pleads. Does he pray for the success of the Confederacy? No! He will stand with his State even to humiliation and death, but no such unconditional prayer for victory escapes his lips. " Thy will be done" is the language of his suit before the throne of the Supreme Ruler.

It was frequently the case that our boys sought the place of guard to farm-houses in the vicinity of camp. The guards, in return for protecting a house, expected food and shelter. One of our men offered his services as guard at a small farm-house; but when he saw the large number of children, and the evident poverty of the family, he regretted the step. The mother of the children, not one of whom was large enough to be useful, told him that on the previous night some soldiers had broken into her house and stolen nearly all her little stock of provisions. Our Parker boy, who had come to feast, remained to work; and as long as the battery camped in the neighborhood, he did the work of a servant on this poor woman's premises.

It was rather embarrassing, even to us rough soldiers, to sleep in the same room with the ladies, as was sometimes the case. Barker, Todd, Richardson, and several others guarded a number of houses one night, two going to each house. At one of these houses the mistress was careful to show the guards the place where she kept her potatoes. " I'm not pertickuler," she explained, " about nothin' but my tater-hole." That, she insisted, must be protected at all hazards. Nor could she be blamed for this.

special solicitude, for potatoes were a very important article of food. At bed-time the two young guards were too modest to take off even their outer garments, as the one apartment of the shanty did not permit a separation of sexes, except by a temporary calico screen.

Had we only thought about it, the farm-houses in that section of Tennessee were not the safest places for a Southern soldier to go to sleep. Men were suspiciously scarce, and the demeanor of the women but too plainly showed their dislike for the boys in gray. Stories of cruelty and outrage perpetrated by "bushwhackers" in the mountains sometimes reached us. These lawless men spared neither Federal nor Confederate, but, taking advantage of the unsettled times, led a wild, predatory life in their mountain fastnesses. They were, however, generally "Union" in their sympathies. It is remarkable that none of our boys ever fell into their clutches. David Brown and a comrade, however, once made a rather narrow escape. They stopped for a while at a farm-house, but the demeanor of the women excited suspicion. On starting to leave, the women insisted upon their remaining, which was so unusual a courtesy that Brown and his comrade became still more uneasy, and left the house. On their way to camp they met a friendly native, who congratulated them on their escape. He said that several men had been known to mysteriously disappear in that house, and it was thought they had been murdered.

A sergeant of Taylor's battery, in charge of a

foraging expedition, suddenly found himself in a
nest of bushwhackers. Finding escape impossible,
he boldly rode up to them, and announced himself
a deserter coming to them. He was riding a fine
horse, which he at once presented to the Captain of
the band. He probably owed his life to this lucky
gift: for during his captivity he overheard many
discussions as to his loyalty, and many propositions
to end the matter by a pistol-shot; but the Captain
always interposed, and his life was spared. During
this time he was privy to several of the engagements
in which the band was concerned, being himself always under guard on those occasions. These "engagements" were simply massacres; for they only
attacked inferior forces or defenceless squads, and
never took any prisoners. After some weeks he
made his escape and rejoined the battalion, with an
experience that could rarely happen, having really
returned from "that bourne from which no traveller
returns."

The 1st day of March, 1864, is memorable in our
annals as the date of one of the most trying marches
the battery ever made. The evening previous we
were posted on an abrupt eminence overlooking the
Nolachucky river, a rapid, brawling tributary of the
Holston. The sky was then overcast with clouds,
and fears were entertained that if much rain fell the
watercourses in our rear would become unfordable.
Our position was considerably in advance of the
main body of the army, and it was feared that the

swollen streams would cut off all retreat should the enemy attack us in large force. These fears were augmented when, towards daybreak, rain commenced to fall rapidly, and with every indication of continuance. Every one knows how soon a mountain rivulet may become a river with the help of a heavy rain. There was a creek about seven miles in our rear which was the main cause of solicitude, and every energy was bent to reach it as soon as practicable. Our road lay through a rude, mountainous section, difficult for artillery under the best circumstances. Now the rains had made our progress still more difficult, and horses and men together could scarcely get the guns over the hills. We were thinly clad, too, and the cold March rain drenched us to the skin.

A difficulty was soon encountered where it was not expected. On reaching a little stream, which nobody had thought of, we found to our amazement that even it was almost impassable, much more the dreaded creek beyond. A four-mule commissary wagon, to instance, driven into it, was immediately whirled to the course of the rushing water, and mules, driver, and wagon went half-swimming, half-walking down the current. The horses to one gun went resolutely enough to the middle of the stream, but there halted; and neither blows nor curses could make them move further. Then came the dreaded command, "Cannoneers to the wheels!" The horses were unhitched, and men took their places, standing waist deep in the water, and some of them even stooping to their chins in the performance of certain parts of duty. Pull! Pull! If the Confederacy succeeds, there is a reward for all this hardship. Perhaps some patriotic poet will shed a tearful verse in memory of our aqueous toils. If not—well, let us pull. But even a "long pull, a strong pull, and a pull altogether" failed to extricate the gun. So the infantry had to help us, and repaid themselves by muttering a few curses about "lazy artillerymen."

It was now after noon, and, although we had been marching since sunrise, we had scarcely travelled five miles, so bad were the roads. We were now over the hills only to get into a morass, which seemed well-nigh bottomless, horses and guns sinking deep at every step, and frequently stopping. Three horses died from exhaustion while we were passing through this morass.

Water, water everywhere, and still a-coming. The darkened heavens seemed exhaustless in their supply, and horses and men could toil but slowly through the mud that gloomy 1st of March. The Parker boys took the matter cheerfully, however, as soldiers generally did. Some of them even sang,—

> " What though the tempest rage ?
>   Heaven is my home.
>   Short is my pilgrimage—
>   Heaven is my home.
>   Time's cold and wintry blast
>   Soon will be overpast ;
>   I shall reach home at last—
>   Heaven is my home."

The creek which was the object of so much solicitude was reached about night-fall. A rough bridge of logs which spanned it was already almost covered by the water, and swaying to and fro with the current. The command came from General Johnson: "Hurry up with the artillery, or we'll lose it!" But the bridge was impassable. To the gloomy features of "night, and storm, and darkness" was added the fear of attack from a powerful enemy in our unprepared condition. "The most miserable hours I ever spent!" said Captain Parker.

At last, about nine o'clock that night, the artillery succeeded in crossing the creek, and encamped a short distance beyond. We arose from our damp beds the next morning to hear it rumored that the enemy, doubting the practicability of retreat in case *we* should advance in force, fell back on the same memorable 1st of March! Thus the two forces employed the day in running from each other!

One day, as we were marching along the road, a lady, on horseback, rode by us. I say, "a lady," and use the word in its more exclusive, if not only proper sense. Plainly but nicely attired, with a countenance that bespoke mingled gentleness and dignity, her whole deportment indicated her conscious right to ladyship. Every hat was lifted as she passed us, and the boys would have rent the air with cheers but for their deep respect for the fair lady's "ear polite." Of course she was "loyal"— to the South!

Among these sort of loyalists the Parker boys
will always rank first and tenderest in their memories the names of Colonel Odell and his wife, and
their three daughters—Virginia, Georgia, and Tennessee. The Colonel had once commanded a Tennessee regiment, but when we met him he was serving the Confederacy as superintendent of some iron
works in Sullivan county. He had also served his
State in the Legislature. Darden and I went to his
house one cold evening and offered our services as
guards. Mrs. Odell kindly accepted us. We were
felicitating ourselves on our good luck, when in
walked a man, at first sight of whom we concluded
he could hold his castle without our aid. Hesitat-
ingly I was proceeding to explain the situation, when
he took both my hands cordially, saying, "Certainly,
sir! Certainly, sir! Go to your camp, and bring
up twenty more of the boys to supper." We then
had the rare pleasure of selecting twenty comrades
to be the guests of the generous Tennessean. His
house was small, but he fed the hungry soldiers
abundantly, and lodged them on the floor and in the
barn. Darden and I were given a bed.

The battalion marched next morning, but en-
camped for a week or more about seven miles from
the Colonel's residence, and not far from Bristol.
We had been in camp only a day or two, when Col.
Odell rode up and asked for Darden and Cannon.
He wanted us to come to his house and stay as long
as the command remained in the neighborhood.
This was in the early spring of 1864, and Captain

Parker would not give permission, as marching orders were expected. Colonel Odell insisting, however, Captain Parker consented for us to go, provided that one of us should report personally to him daily. So each day, for more than a week, Darden or I rode fourteen miles (the distance going and returning) simply to say to Captain Parker, "Here I am." We were quite willing to do this, however, as the Colonel and his family were very kind, and did all they could to make our stay at their house quite pleasant.

During this period furloughs were given to several classes of soldiers. To capture a deserter, to obtain a new recruit, or to get married, entitled the fortunate "Johnny Reb" to a two-weeks' furlough. One of our boys (John Glenn) went to Richmond to get married, and came back singularly wretched. In fact, Captain Parker put him on "double duty" for coming back single. Darden and I captured a deserter, and let him escape, and all through the sharpness of one of those Tennessee Union women. We had the deserter safe and sound; he only wanted to go to his sister's house and get his clothes. Once there, his sister spread her table with tempting food, and we sat down to dine—the deserter seated with us. His sister seemed to be very hospitable, and pressed us to eat heartily. The deserter about this time left the table and stood in the doorway. His sister in the meanwhile talked incessantly and proffered various articles of food. I looked to the door again, and the deserter was gone! Even then we did not immediately get up. It looked rude and ungrateful. Presently we sprang from our seats and ran to the door, only to see our deserter already far into the woods on the hillside, with our two-weeks' furlough rapidly disappearing with his re-treating heels!

I recollect that I felt very much impressed that afternoon as to the vanity of human wishes, and so forth. A cat who has just let slip a captured mouse might appreciate my feelings.

We were very much ashamed to have been thus outwitted, and spent the following two days in try-ing to recapture our prisoner. The first night we lodged in a little shanty on the road-side, where there was a man and his wife, and quite a numerous offspring. The man claimed to be a rheumatic; hence his civilian attire. At supper we all sat around a pot of potatoes, which was on the hearth, with salt convenient, and eat—potatoes, and potatoes. If I paused in eating, my hospitable host would promptly say, "Won't you take another ta-*ter*, sir?" And then he would kindly pass the salt. How delicious that supper! How truly polite was that illiterate backwoodsman! I went to sleep that night thinking about his poverty and his numerous family, and— "Won't you take another ta-*ter*, sir?"

The next morning, on leaving, we gave the poor man a gold dollar. He was surprised and overjoyed. My mother had supplied me with a little gold to be used on special occasions, and I thought an occasion had arisen.

That day Darden and I passed through Papers-ville, hunting for the deserter. We learned that he had relatives living in Washington county, Virginia, and inferred that he might have gone to them. About noon we crossed the State line, and at night stopped at the house of a wealthy gentleman, where we met a number of Morgan's men. We confided our business to Mr. ———, our host, and he offered to guide us to the house where we supposed the deserter might have taken refuge. The rain poured in torrents, and it was so dark that we followed only the sound of our guide's footfalls.

Arriving at the house, we knocked at the door.

"You shan't come in here, stranger," answered a woman's voice.

It was only a log house, with chinks between the logs, through which I could see that there were only two persons in the room, both women; but one of them was young and very strongly built. She had in her hand an iron poker, firmly grasped; and there was a look in her face that "meant business." I was satisfied that the deserter was not there; but what would the boys think if, added to the escape of the deserter, they should hear that one woman had barred our "right of search"?

So we stood at the door and tried to convince this plucky young girl that our intentions were lawful and peaceable.

At last, after a long parley, she said:

"Now, look here, stranger! I'm a goin' to let you in here now! But if you tries to do anything wrong, me or you's got to die one, stranger!"

The door was then cautiously opened, and Darden and I, dripping wet, walked to the blazing wood-fire and stood a few minutes. Our heroine (for such she was, and of the truest) eyed us suspiciously as we passed her, and then her manner softened, and, when we started to go, she asked us to stay longer and warm ourselves. This we could not do, as our guide was outside in the storm waiting for us. The writer is sorry that he cannot give the name of this Virginia mountain girl, who, though living in a log hut, was ready to defend her honor with her life.

In February, 1864, Colonel Alexander was formally commissioned as Brigadier-General, and Col. Frank Huger succeeded to the command of the battalion.

"Drive on, Abram!" How the battalion yelled these words as they saw the horses of the headquarters wagon begin to move! "This way, Abram!" and the head of column turned to right or left, the whole battalion following the lead of General Alexander's driver of said wagon. This was on the march, of course, and not when advancing into battle. The General, though a West Pointer, had this peculiar way of giving orders through a negro servant. This "historian" dares express the wish that the "Father of the faithful" may say "This way!" to General Alexander when he shall have completed life's journey, and take him to his "bosom," or at least to some region more hospitable to Confederate soldiers than was East Tennessee!

The Tennessee campaign, with its varied experiences, was now drawing to a close, and with it the boy company completed its second year of service in the Confederate armies. We were now about to return to Virginia, once more to face our old antagonists of the Army of the Potomac; but in this, the last year of the great struggle, we were destined to fight, not only vastly superior numbers in front, but starvation in rear.

Near Bristol, Lieutenant Saville was taken sick, and on the way to Richmond he died, and was buried at Liberty, in Bedford county. " One of the most faultless men I ever knew," said Captain Parker. Quiet and taciturn, he rose by merit from the ranks to a lieutenantcy ; and, whether in camp or field, he was the same polite, practical, dutiful man.

Since the war I have stood near the humble mound that marks his last resting-place. Not far away the Peaks of Otter rise tall and lonely among the everlasting hills. It was a morning in June; a soft south wind was blowing, and a field of wheat was bending before it, making billows of living green that shimmered in the sunlight. I looked to the grave, and thought of the words of Saint Paul, "That which thou sowest is not quickened except it die." I looked to the Peaks, which cast a gloomy shadow over the hills below, and I wept over the awful mystery of death. But presently the birds

13

were singing their gayest notes; a streamlet was
murmuring its ceaseless lullaby; and the summer
winds, as they toyed gently with the waving wheat,
seemed to whisper, "God is the God of smiles as
well as of tears."

My mother had given me, as I said, a little gold,
to be used in urgent contingencies. Ah! how significant were those little gold pieces! How much
more than I appreciated! How they could have
whispered of self-denial and undying love if my
dull ears had only listened! If the yellow metal
itself was precious, how divinely rich was the motive
of the giver! Blessed is the man who imbibes his
ideal of womanhood from the bosom of a good mother! To him all womanhood is holy, and immortal
love a fact against which the waves of sin and doubt
shall beat in vain. For him reformation is always
possible, no matter into what depths of sin and misery he may have fallen; for the light of that pure
life will shine like a star in the darkness, and lead
him to look up towards his MOTHER and his GOD!

CHAPTER XI.

FROM SPOTSYLVANIA TO APPOMATTOX.

" There lives a Judge
To whose all-pondering mind a noble aim,
Faithfully kept, is as a noble deed ;
In whose pure sight all virtue doth succeed."

THE last year of the war between the States, though the most tragic and eventful of the four, is historically the least interesting, except as it exhibits the force of superior skill and equal courage against " overwhelming numbers and resources." Up to the time that General Grant took command of the Army of the Potomac there was a spirit of chivalry about the war, as when equal foes meet in brave and doubtful contest. When, however, after three years of arduous struggle, the Southern soldier saw the already thinned ranks of the Confederate armies becoming weaker and yet weaker, and the hosts of the enemy growing daily in numbers and enthusiasm, the shadows of coming defeat assumed palpable shape in the not distant future, and the struggle became one more of honor than of hope.

This was the time that " tried men's souls "—that proved the stuff that their patriotism was made of. Those who, three years before, had favored secession because they thought it would *pay* (miserable knaves!)

finding their selfish calculations wide of the mark, skulked far from the sounds of unprofitable strife; or, if compelled by conscription to stand with their countrymen upon the frequent battlefields, served rather to weaken the veterans by their timidity and melancholy. Those who had drawn the sword in the spirit of adventure or selfish ambition were equally disappointed; for hunger, peril, and death became monotonously common facts, and required the sternest principle to face them calmly.

There were, however, to their honor be it written, a determined minority of the Southern people who, though of different political antecedents, honestly and bravely stood to their colors. These, in spite of an unwise administration at Richmond—in spite of the army of speculators and knaves in their rear, and in spite of the apparently hopeless task of successfully opposing the ever-increasing hosts in their front,—these loyal men, cheered by heroic women, and led by that pure and gallant patriot LEE, looked steadily upward and forward, and marched, if to defeat, still not to dishonor.

The sun was just peeping above the horizon as the battalion, under Colonel Frank Huger, moved down the quiet country road. What a sweet spring day! How fresh and soothing the morning air! And how calm the woods on either side of the road, save when the birds trill their untutored music! Even the bosom of poor old battle-scarred Virginia thrills in the embrace of returning summer. Trees, blackened and torn in the storms of former battles, again put forth their tender, green leaves, and daisies are growing where but lately the hostile rider spurred his horse to the charge.

Hark! What sound is that?—full, heavy, solemn—breaking the peaceful stillness? Again and again it falls upon the ear; Lee and Grant are face to face, and the great battle of the Wilderness has begun.

"Ah, Captain," said Dr. Monteiro, our battalion surgeon, riding up to Captain Parker, "Ah, Captain, distance lends enchantment to the sound, as well as to the view, I think!"

Such was the nature of the ground that but little artillery could be used in the battle of the Wilderness, and our battalion, though on the field and ready for action, was not engaged. All day long we listened to the roar of musketry in the wilderness. We heard that Longstreet was wounded, and a shadow of gloom was cast over our hearts. All day long we listened, if haply we might tell, by the nearing or receding sounds, whether our brave infantry were holding their own.

In the immediately subsequent battle of Spotsylvania Court-House the battalion took a prominent part, and was complimented by General Lee himself. The position occupied was one of peculiar importance, being at an angle of the line, from which we could enfilade the charging Federals to our left. On our right we were supported by Kershaw's infantry, and from that direction the enemy enfiladed

us; but the nature of the ground prevented their
fire from being very destructive. Their sharpshooters, however, advanced to within forty-five yards of
our position, and, sheltering themselves in rifle-pits,
would try to pick off our cannoneers. Of course,
when not firing, every man "lay low."

It was probably during one of the first days of
this "battle array," and when the enemy's sharpshooters had not become very troublesome, that I
saw one of Kershaw's men needlessly exposing himself.

"Comrade," said I, "why don't you lie down?"
You'll get hit presently."

"Damn 'em, they can't hit me!" was his defiant
reply.

It was not long before this "cool spell" was succeeded by a heavy shower of bullets. Still we were
not ordered to rise up, and I was curious to notice
whether Kershaw's man maintained his proud per-
pendicular. But no; the "tall," if not "reverend
head," was lying as low as ours. "Comrade," said
I, "why don't you stand up? 'Damn 'em, they
can't hit' you!' He looked, rather than spoke, his
reply. He must have been a new recruit.

On the 10th of May there was heavy fighting.
The enemy charged the lines repeatedly to our immediate left, under cover of woods, while their
sharpshooters kept up an annoying fusilade in front.
Their artillery also raked us from the right. Un-
daunted by all this, Parker trained his four rifled-guns
so as to enfilade the enemy as they charged through

the woods to our left. He was careful to send a
sergeant to that part of the line to watch the effect
of our shots. Limbs from the trees were thus cut
down upon the enemy, and our firing was probably
never so destructive as on that day. The infantry
told us that the Federal lines sometimes broke under
it before they could get a shot.

It was on this day that Lieutenant Brown and
Stafford Parker were wounded. One of those rascally sharpshooters did the job for our brave lieutenant, and a piece of shell deprived young Parker
of an arm. As Brown fell, the blood spurted from
an ugly hole in his neck, and we all thought that
the wound was mortal.

It was a risky thing, by the way, to go to the rear
with wounded men, or for any purpose. It was
rising ground, and in full view of the sharpshooters.
The men who carried Brown to the rear were exposed to their fire, and were about to drop the
stretcher, when Billy Parr, a brave fellow, drew his
pistol and compelled them to do their duty.

Both Brown and Parker survived their serious
wounds, the former serving as Captain and the latter
as Lieutenant at the close of hostilities.

As we faced Grant on the Spotsylvania line for
nearly a week, the infantry in the trenches were
sometimes relieved by fresh troops. On one of
these occasions, Captain Parker, seeing a regiment
running to the rear, rushed after them, and called
loudly to them to come back and stand to their duty.
He supposed the lines had been broken and his guns

would be captured. "We are relieved!" one of these men took time to say, to the infinite relief of our anxious commander.

How did we get anything to eat during that long week of harassing days and sleepless nights? That question introduces to the reader Mr. Thomas W. Pemberton, our commissary sergeant. The cooking was done in the rear under his supervision. Though supplies were scant, the management of our commissariat was admirable during the last year of the war. Especially was "Cousin Sallie" careful to feed her champions when they stood in line of battle. The corn bread and fried bacon she dispensed might not compare as elegant diet with the cheese and coffee and canned beef of her rich old relative "Uncle Sam," but, like Goldsmith's hermit, she gave it "with good will." A welcome visitor was "Uncle Tommy," as we fondly called Sergeant Pemberton, when, after running the gauntlet of the Federal sharpshooters, he tumbled into the trenches with a bag full of meat and bread.

"Pass it down the line : Enemy advancing !"

These words were often heard during the night. The warning would be taken up, as designed, and a voice farther on would repeat, "Pass it down the line : enemy advancing !" until the sounds grew faint and yet fainter, as they passed from lip to lip along the long line of sleepless soldiers. I say, "sleepless," but several times I dozed, while standing as No. 3 with my thumb on the touch-hole of the gun.

Early on the morning of the 12th we were startled by a terrific crash of musketry on the line to our right.　It turned out that the enemy had broken through General Edward Johnson's division, and captured nearly all of it.　In driving back the Federals and rectifying our lines the Confederates did some of the most magnificent fighting of the war; and never did the character of General Lee show more grandly great than on that day when he saw sudden and overwhelming disaster staring him in the face.

Thus, for nearly a week, the Parker boys did their part in repulsing General Grant on the Spotsylvania line.　They were never relieved by another battery, but borrowed ammunition when their own was exhausted.

"Some curious incidents happened at Spotsylvania," writes Sam Weisiger, of Georgia; "notably one on the last night we spent on those lines.　Our picket line was not put out during the day, as the enemy's pickets were so close to us as to render such action unnecessarily hazardous; but at night a picket was placed every fifty yards in the ditch just over the works.　That night the picket in front of the battery said he heard the Yankee picket say they would charge at one o'clock that night.　Our officers immediately notified the men not to fall asleep, but to keep on the alert until that hour.　Our guns were double-shotted with canister, friction-primers inserted, and every man stood at his post for some three hours in a misty drizzle of most uncomfortable rain.

The hour came and passed, but no charge. After a little, our officers allowed the men to take short naps, or to 'sleep with one eye open.' The day broke, and everything looked about as it did the night before. The smoke of the camp-fires arose beyond the Yankee works; but to one rebel's gaze, at least, matters looked suspicious. A tall Georgian, in Tige Anderson's brigade, suddenly exclaimed, 'I'm darned ef I b'lieve anybody's over thar! I'm goin' ter see!' He sprung up on the works, gun in hand. The Yankees rose and fired at him, and then took to their heels. The mystery was solved: Grant had retired at one o'clock, instead of charging, and then commenced his everlasting flank movement. Following the gallant Georgian, our men rushed toward the Yankee lines in a mass. Over them we went, but found soon that, like a retreating tiger, Grant had claws. He had not moved far nor rapidly, and immediately threw out a line of battle to check our advance. Then we did halt very suddenly ; nor was that all : we scampered back to our works, and formed properly, and followed 'old Marse Robert' as he kept between Grant and Richmond."

At North Anna River and Hanover Junction we again disputed Grant's right of way to Richmond. At the latter place Lamartine Sieker, a new and youthful recruit, did a brave thing in a very cool manner. The men wanted water, and the only spring convenient was between us and the enemy. It looked like certain death to attempt to reach that spring, and we were amazed when this new recruit offered to go there. With a half-dozen canteens strung around him, he not only went to the spring, but returned, looking as gay and careless as if he had enjoyed the perilous errand.

At Hanover Junction a rise in the ground in front of our works prevented the third gun, of which Jim Darden was corporal, from having a fair shot at the enemy. Captain Parker decided to advance this gun beyond our line, and post it on the obstructing eminence. The gun was moved out, and the detachment began to throw up a redoubt. We saw Darden's eyes roll and snap—not from fear (there was none braver than he, Heaven rest his soul!)—but he looked at the redoubt, and then at the line behind us, which was filled with Hood's gallant veterans, and then he spoke. "Captain." said he, "this will never do. We are set up here for a target for both sides. If the enemy ever gets in the vicinity of this redoubt, not a man will live to tell he took part in this fight." Looking at it calmly, in the light of later events, we see the wisdom of Darden's views. Luckily, no fight took place at that particular part of the line; but if there had, and it had become necessary to withdraw our gun, not a man would have survived.

During this campaign, when the incessant fighting and marching had turned night into day, and we had hardly time even to eat, we were joined by the battalion of heavy artillery which had been stationed for a long time in the defence-line of Richmond. They had seen no active service, and one of our boys asked a private of this battalion how long they would stay with us. "I don't know," was the sincere reply; "but we can't stay over Sunday anyhow, for we didn't bring any clean clothes with us"!

Soon after the battle of Cold Harbor, on the 3d of June, 1864, I saw General Lee. He was riding slowly past our battalion, which had halted on the roadside. He was apparently in deep abstraction, his head slightly bowed, and eyes seeming not to range beyond his horse's mane. He himself was probably then in doubt as to the next move of his great antagonist. There was in the battalion a simple-witted fellow nicknamed Possum. This man planted himself in front of General Lee, and, looking up into his face, grinned and said, "Howdy do, dad?" General Lee, roused from his reverie, looked up, and, in a kindly sad voice, answered, "Howdy do, my man?" and rode on.

Soon after this, with Pickett's division, we crossed to the south side of the James. In the evening the enemy shelled us from their gunboats. Far into the night they continued to send these monster shells; but they did not get our range fairly, and we went to sleep notwithstanding the hideous noise.

Some time after midnight the sleeping drivers and cannoneers were aroused. Horses were hitched to the pieces, and stealthily we moved through the darkness and took possession of the line of breastworks facing Bermuda Hundreds. About a mile to our left was Howlett's Bluff, where the Confederates had a battery of heavy artillery, commanding the river at that point. To our right the line extended to Fort Clifton, on the Appomattox.

It was when we had just taken possession of this line that I heard a good word spoken for General B. F. Butler—and by a lady. Her house was situated within the range of gunboat shells, and she was preparing to leave it when I met her. She told me that when General Butler was in the neighborhood, about the time of his fight with Beauregard, he rode up one evening and asked permission to make her house his headquarters. She replied, coldly, that he had the power to do as he pleased. To this General Butler dissented, saying that he would not use her house without her permission. He was so polite, she said, that she received him and his staff as guests for the night. Before departing, in the morning, he particularly inquired if anything was missing, and, if so, offering to pay for it. He hoped, he said, that this Virginia lady would not think Gen. Butler to be such a very bad man.

This reminds me of the story about the good old lady who would never speak evil of anybody. Some children, knowing her charitable disposition, teasingly asked her, "Grandma, what is your opinion of the devil?" "Well, my dears," said she, after a little reflection, "I think we might all imitate his perseverance!" This old lady, however, could not have been the same who complimented General Butler, for my recollection is that she was yet in the bloom of early womanhood.

In this house Mrs. Parker, the wife of our gallant

Captain, lived for more than six months. It was scarcely a mile from the battery, and though huge gunboat shells sometimes made ugly holes in the ground round about, this plucky lady chose to reside there and share some of the dangers, if not the comforts, of soldier life. Our Captain was eminently practical. As a physician, in nearly all our marches he had an ambulance, which was politely supposed to contain only medical supplies; but there were skeptics who saw, or thought they saw, "good things," both to eat and wear, stored away in said "ambulam," or "avalanche," as its driver variously termed it. To this was added a cow, and Parker's ambulance and Parker's cow became notorious adjuncts of the Army of Northern Virginia. It was funny, on the march, to see this cow solemnly trudging along the road with the thousands of soldiers and horses,—perhaps the only creature of her *kind* in all that vast host. Though she might have lacked congenial company, she could not have felt lonely; for the infantry, especially, would yell vociferously at the sight of her, and make all sorts of witty remarks. But milk was a good thing to have on the camp-board, and our provident Captain bore all jokes on the subject quite pleasantly. While on the Howlett line he procured another cow; and though provender was scarce, and these kine soon rivalled Pharoah's in their leanness, they played a very useful part in this unique domestic life on the lines.

As week after week rolled away we strengthened our fortifications, until they were impregnable. Unlike the trenches around Petersburg, where there was almost continuous fighting, whole weeks passed away with scarcely a shot from either side. The James river was only a mile from our position, and to it we often resorted to bathe. The season was dry, and the water clear and deep, and sometimes as many as a hundred "rebs" might be seen thus disporting themselves within deadly range of the "Yankee" batteries. Such was the good understanding between us and "our friends, the enemy," that they never fired upon us; and our heavy guns on the bluff extended the same courtesy to their bathers in the river below.

Intercourse between Federals and Confederates became so common that it was made the subject of official interdict. They frequently met in the woods between the lines, and traded for newspapers, tobacco, coffee, etc.

Federal gunners were not so considerate to some of our fellows who went into a sorghum field commanded by their pieces. Rations were very short; one could easily eat his day's allowance at a meal; and some of these hungry men were chewing the sorghum stalks, when a Federal battery opened on them and killed one and wounded several.

Something similar to this, and more destructive, was afterwards done on our side. General Pickett rode up to one of our batteries, and asked for its commander. On Captain O. B. Taylor answering the call, General Pickett pointed to a group of Federals lounging under the shade of the trees opposite, some of them playing cards, and evidently fully trusting to the tacit truce prevailing.

"Can you put a shell in that party?" asked Pickett.

"I can, General; but there will be no peace here for days to come."

"Do it," said Pickett.

The gun was carefully aimed, and the deadly missile exploded fairly in the midst of these careless players. As Taylor expected, there was no peace on that part of the line for days to come. Federal cannon roared again and again, and in every way possible the enemy tried to make life miserable, if not brief, for the Confederates.

On the left the Parker Battery was supported by the Fifteenth Virginia infantry, and on the right by the Seventeenth Virginia, under Colonel Herbert. The Fifteenth was mostly recruited from Richmond city and adjacent counties, and the Seventeenth from Alexandria and vicinity. The social relations between these regiments and the Parker boys were quite intimate, especially in religious matters, which, in this prolonged camp, became a prominent feature. We not only built little houses for ourselves, but a bomb-proof church—at least, we so called it; but, like our "so-called Confederate government," its immunity from damage would hardly be respected by a determined Yankee shell, especially of the mortar variety. We dug several feet into the ground, and constructed a roof that would turn water. Rude benches were made, and a stand for the preacher. A choir, called the "Bull-Frog Club," with Buck Jones as "striker," led the singing. Here the good chaplain, Philip F. August, and others, preached to the soldiers, and consoled them with the "comfortable assurance" of a "reasonable religious hope."

Sometimes there were meetings at which any one so disposed was invited to make "a few remarks." On one of these occasions a brother rose and said: "My brethren, I'se got nothin' agin nobody, and I hope nobody's got nothin' agin me." In spite of the double negatives in this text, we interpreted him as saying that his sentiments were pacific toward mankind in general, and he hoped that they were reciprocated. He then shuffled his feet and twisted his arms, and repeated the same words. No more would he say. No one could deny that the sentiment was good, though a trifle too catholic for the times. This ludicrous speech I recollect, but not one word of the grand sermons of Joseph Stiles, who preached to us repeatedly.

The beginning of a prayer, offered by one of the men, I distinctly remember. In a clear but trembling voice, he said: "O LORD, we thank Thee that Thou hast said, 'As the mountains are round about Jerusalem, so the Lord is round about His people from henceforth even for ever.'" Then followed an address to the Throne of Grace, gentle and pathetic, and breathing a spirit of utmost trustfulness in the sleepless Guardian of His people's weal. The man was Tom Royall, who, Mr. August thought, ought to be a preacher.

14

Another scene rises clearly defined in the vista of
the past. An infantry company is marching to the
tap of the drum. "Halt!" and they stand at "parade rest" near a cluster of trees, through which the
rays of the setting sun are broken into a thousand
golden glories. A man steps out from the ranks
and reads from the sacred Book. "The LORD is my
shepherd; I shall not want. He maketh me to lie
down in green pastures; He leadeth me beside the
still waters." Oh, how sweetly sounded those dear
old Saxon heart-words! How tenderly the twilight
shadows fell over all, as, kneeling there, the words
of prayer were borne on angel pinions to the
skies.

Among the impromptu addresses made in this
underground meeting-place was one which deeply
impressed me. Tom Royall had prayed, when a
man rose and spoke somewhat after this fashion:
"My friends, we all know the trials and terrors of
soldier life. Separated from wife, or child, or mother, while perhaps they are wanting the very necessaries of life; ourselves enduring the pangs of hunger and thirst, the weariness of the march, and daily
exposed to wounds and death. All this we endure—
all this we brave—all this for a government that at
best must pass away with the ages, as do all things
finite; but God offers us citizenship in a kingdom
that is everlasting, under a government that is perfect, and in a country which is fairer than poet's
most gorgeous dream; and yet how feeble are our
efforts to gain that glorious prize!"

Surely, steadily, the superior numbers and resources of the North were reducing the Confederacy
to its death-struggles.   Such men in our company as
Darden, an original secessionist and the soul of
honor, gave up all hope after the fall of Atlanta.
Desertions were so frequent and numerous that
picket-firing on the lines was more frequently caused
by that than by an advance of the enemy.   "Die-in-
the-ditch resolutions," as they were called, were read
to our company, and all pledged themselves to be
"faithful unto the last."

The Government finally ordered out the last reserves.   These recruits did much to dispirit the veteran Confederates.   They came in citizens' clothes,
and their rueful countenances and sad talk was anything but helpful to the old soldiers, who had learned
to be gay even in the presence of hardship and danger.   "Where are the volunteers?" asked a British
recruiting officer in the Scottish highlands.   "All
safe," was the response; "they are tied up in the
barn."   These were the kind of volunteers that reinforced our Southern army of liberty in the dark
days of the last year of the war.

If food for the men was scarce, forage for the
horses was even scarcer.   These poor creatures, picketed in the woods in our rear, gnawed the trees in
their hunger, whinnied, and died by hundreds.   This
was the reason why our veteran battalion was left on
the comparatively quiet Howlett line, when Pickett
went to join in the more important struggle around
Petersburg.

There were some stacks of fodder in the lowlands near the river, which were commanded by Federal guns. It was impracticable to get this forage for our starving horses during the day, but it was determined to make an effort under cover of darkness. A detail of mounted men started after midnight. Just as the detail moved off, my horse's saddle-girth broke, and I was thus delayed until the other men had gotten at least a mile ahead. The route lay through some swampy woods which had been the scene of conflict between Generals Butler and Beauregard. I had been through these woods in the day-time, and seen the bones of half-buried men portruding from shallow graves, and human bones dangling from pine-twigs, where, even at high noon, the sun could shed but a shadowed light. As this little raid involved some danger, I was compelled to ride alone through these gloomy woods, or become liable to the suspicion of shirking duty. When I reached the darkest point of the ride, where the road was flanked by sluggish swamp-water, I peered eagerly into the thickets on either side, thinking surely, if ever I am to see a " ghost," now is the time and this the place. My mind was so penetrated with this idea that I determined to reduce my horse's pace to a walk, fearing that if I galloped through these ghostly shades my imagination would conjure into palpable shape some of its own pictures. Thus I rode slowly along for perhaps a mile, looking and listening, and thinking of what I had seen in these woods during the day ; but no sound did I hear, save the hooting of an owl, and no sight but the dark outline of trees stretching their leafless arms over the sleepers who had fought their last battle.

Our boys succeeded in capturing the forage.

Eloquent orators, both clerical and lay, were sent to the front, to cheer by gallant words the drooping hopes of the men. Among others was Governor Vance, of North Carolina, of whom a good story is told. He was riding near the army, on a lean, slow horse, when he saw just ahead of him an animal of the *genus homo* variety who moved even more slowly than Vance's horse. The witty Governor instinctively recognized him as a brother " Tar-heel," and said kindly, " You needn't move, my good man; *I* won't run over you." " I know you won't run over me," was the drawling response, "but I don't want to be gored to death by a pack of bones!"

If the Virginians called the Carolinians "tar-heels," and joked them about " sticking," they retorted by calling the Virginians "sore-backs." They said that at Gaines' Mill the Carolinians charged the enemy over the backs of the prostrate Virginians; hence the name "sore-backs." This scrap of history is given on the authority of that gallant "Tarhelian," James Howland, now a citizen of New York.

In was about February, 1865, that Captain Parker announced to his men that any who chose to do so might cut wood in the lowlands near the river, and his brother (Captain John H. Parker, of the C. S.

Navy) would convey it by boats to Richmond. At that time fuel, as well as provisions, was scarce in Richmond, and a number of the men accepted the offer of our thoughtful Captain. Among others, George Jones and the writer cut wood for several days to send to our mothers in the beleaguered capital. The weather being cold, and our rations inadequate, the violent exercise of wood-chopping made us very hungry. Thus weakened, we would stop work and drink water plentifully, and ply the axe again. In spite of all difficulties, we piled up several cords in the swamps, fondly hoping that the dear ones at home would enjoy at least the comfort of a ruddy blaze as the fruit of our toil; but this wood never reached them, and in a short while the city itself was destined to be fuel for a conflagration that would darken the noon-day skies with its smoke.

Furloughs were "few and far between." During three years of service in the boy battery, only two weeks was I absent from its guns—that is, legally; but stolen visits to Richmond were frequent, especially from the Howlett line. It may be "telling tales out of school," but these trips were often made with the connivance of our officers. The compact between officer and man was, "You may miss two or three roll-calls, but, if you are caught, you in honor bind yourself not to say I gave you permission." Thus, with all safe in the rear, our boys (a few at a time) made many a successful "on to Richmond" movement. Richardson, Henry Tyler, and

I made one of the last of these stolen visits to the fated capital. Tyler, I remember, when annoyed, would say "Dod bam it," which peculiar language impressed me as being a very shrewd evasion of the law against profanity. Through his influence with a certain general officer on the north bank of the James, we reached safely the eastern suburbs of Richmond. As Richardson neared his home, he stamped his foot, exclaiming, "Macgregor treads his own heather again!" This was the last time we saw the "old folks at home" before the great battles that ended the meteor career of the Confederacy. There were other, however, than old folks whom we saw, you may readily imagine, gentle reader. The picture of a fair-haired maiden of fifteen summers, her modest blue eyes rivalling in purity the vernal skies lingers fondly in memory; and we could not soon forget the sylph-like form of "gentle ANNIE." (The angels of the artists always have fair hair and blue eyes, which has led some one to say that "only blue-eyed people go to heaven"; but this cannot be true, for my "beautiful Emma," in a former chapter, had dark eyes.)

About one o'clock on Sunday morning, the 2d of April, 1865, we were aroused from our slumbers by the rapid discharge of picket guns, and every cannoneer ran to his post. For an hour or more the enemy fired furiously, the shells lighting up the night with their bright performances. Suddenly all was quiet again, and we lay down to sleep.

Day was just reddening the east when a crash of musketry from the pickets again called us to our feet. Scarcely had we time to man our pieces when the enemy carried the picket line and were rushing on us. Bang! bang! bang! went the cannon in rapid succession, with a roar of small arms on either flank. The advance of the Federals was scarcely more, after all, than a heavy demonstration. Finding us strong enough to repulse them, they gave up the task of carrying our lines after about an hour of fruitless effort.

About dusk that evening, amidst profound quiet, we proceed to withdraw our pieces, and move cautiously to the rear. No one seems to know where we are going. Some say that we are going to Petersburg to reinforce the troops there; but it is soon evident from the direction we march that Petersburg is not our objective point, nor Richmond. On we move, along melancholy swampy roads, plodding wearily in the darkness. We encamp towards morning near Chesterfield Court-house, and awake from an hour's fitful sleep to hear the thunder of the explosions that tell that Richmond has fallen!

As day advances the northern horizon is darkened by smoke. Brave Richmond is in flames! Mother, wife, sisters are there; but we follow Robert Lee.

Marching all that day as fast as our famished horses could be driven, we encamped again at night. That was the last night that the dear old company ever slept together. At morning roll-call a number of men did not answer to their names. Major Parker made us an address, in which, with tearful eloquence, he alluded to these recreant ones, and urged us that remained to be true to the last.

Some time previous to this, Major Parker, having completed three years' service with us, had accepted promotion, and Lieutenant J. Thompson Brown succeeded to the captaincy of the battery.

To those who had read of Napoleon's retreat from Moscow, our retreat toward Appomattox had many features in common; but especially did Sheridan and Custer remind us of the Cossacks. They would with their splendidly armed cavalry make sudden swoops upon our wearied and half-starved lines, gobble up a wagon or a gun, and a few men and horses; sweep off in widening circles, only to return again, when a favorable opportunity presented itself, and renew their harassing attacks.

At Amelia Court-house the battalion was divided. The best horses and guns and the veteran cannoneers were put into a command by themselves, hot work being expected. Colonel Frank Huger had command of this veteran division, and Major Parker of the other. We marched all that night, suffering greatly from hunger and fatigue, and about three o'clock of the next day, participated in the battle of Sailors' Creek. In this last fight of the Army of Northern Virginia nearly all of this half-battalion, with about five thousand infantry, was captured. The other division of the battalion, under Major Parker, surrendered with General Lee, on the 9th of April, 1865.

See that man in dust-covered gray, as he nears the once proud capital of the Confederacy. Its steeples, save one, still point to the skies, and around many of its loveliest homes the flowers of spring are exhaling their sweetest odors; but all of its stateliest stores and factories are in ashes, and where bridges once spanned the James, the beautiful river murmurs mournfully against the separated sentinel piers. Even the trees around the Capitol Park have been blackened by the great fire of the 3d of April, and there are miles of streets where only tottering walls mark the spots where thrifty merchants once held sway.

Our man in gray walks briskly along one of these ruined avenues of commerce. He himself is beggared by the defeat of the Confederacy; but though there is a natural stoop in his shoulders, his step is proud, and his eyes gleam strong and clear.

A man in citizens' dress walks up to our man in gray, and inquires,—

"Major, what about Robert? He has not returned, and mother is very uneasy."

"Robert? Ah, yes. You needn't be uneasy about him; he's true. [Pausing.] I hope none of those deserters will presume to speak to me."

"He's true." It matters not, it seems, whether Robert is living or dead; but "he's true!" Who would aspire to a grander epitaph?

This man in gray is Major Parker, the commander of the boy company. No faultless hero he, but a man of Roman honor, unconquered and unconquerable,—a true type of the best of those who followed Lee the immortal.

Thus closes the scene. It is not without pride that I point to the career of Parker's battery. On its battle-flag might be written a long list of historic fields where it played no unworthy part. Manassas Plains, Sharpsburg, Fredericksburg, Marye's Hill, Chancellorsville, Gettysburg, Chattanooga, Knoxville, Spotsylvania, and a number of lesser places heard the thunder of its guns, and never were they driven.

Is it all in vain? The weary marchings and fastings, the stubborn struggles of blood-stained fields, the wounds, the tears, the deaths,—are they all in vain? Some are. Perish the wrong, whether hid beneath Southern gray or Northern blue! But the right never fails. It is as indestructible as God! Every labor performed with noble motive hath its sure reward; every tear of pure sympathy is exhaled towards the skies; every pain, every death, that hath the love of truth in it, will live with cross-crowned Calvary!

CHAPTER XII.

POINT LOOKOUT.

"Home! Alas! what did a defeated Confederate have to do with a home? All his hopes dead; his beloved flag forever furled; Lee's sword forever sheathed; and his bleeding Southland sitting in sackcloth and ashes, a Niobe among the nations!"
--Private S. P. Weisiger.

SURRENDER, you d——d rebel!"

A Yankee cavalryman is holding an uplifted sabre over Robert Cannon's head as he stands defenceless near the now captured guns of the boy company.

"I surrender," quickly replies Robert; for there is a look in the Yankee's eyes that is anything but friendly.

"Did your gun kill that man?" says the Yankee, motioning to a spot in the woods where lay a mutilated corpse in blue. The sabre is still uplifted, and, as rebel and Yankee now see eye to eye, the rebel knows that upon his answer depends his life.

"My gun has not fired a shot," says Robert, and looks his captor squarely in the eyes.

The sabre is slowly lowered, and the stern look is succeeded by one of compassion.

"Johnny, ain't you mighty hungry?"

"I'm nearly dead," answers Robert.

Custer's man—for such he was—then gave Robert some crackers, and led him a short distance to the rear, where General Custer was directing the assault on Lee's thin line of starving patriots. Robert, as he stood near Custer, knew not but what he was the only man (save Kirtley) that was a prisoner. The fact was, however, that nearly all of Huger's men and guns had been taken by a sudden swoop of the enemy's cavalry; and that, too, before some of the guns had a chance to fire a shot, and when not a bayonet of our gallant infantry was in supporting distance.

Robert Cannon had been standing near Custer only a few minutes when these captured Confederates came pouring in, among them Colonel Huger and Captain Brown.

"How are you, Huger!" cried Custer, as our Colonel came up.

Custer and Huger had been cadets together at West Point, and this was their first meeting after many years. His captor had stolen Huger's hat and watch; but the gallant Colonel had emptied every chamber of his revolver into the Federals before he surrendered. We heard also that Captain Taylor refused to surrender, and died fighting, his body being riddled by bullets.

General Custer proposed to Huger and Brown, that if they would remain with him temporarily, he would send a staff officer for two horses for their use. This offer Huger declined, but at Brown's suggestion he accepted. The horses were brought, and General Custer and our two Confederates rode to an eminence from which a portion of Pickett's men, formed in line of battle five hundred yards away, were distinctly seen.

"Frank," said Custer, "what men are those?"

"If I were to tell you," quickly replied Huger, "I would not only forfeit your respect, but abuse my own self-respect. I can only suggest that you find out for yourself."

"Well, I will do so," answered Custer, laughing, "and show you gentlemen how I take in you rebs out of the wet."

Custer then ordered a body of cavalry to "go down and bring in those men." The charge was made, but repulsed, and so close did that thin line of "rebel" infantry come to the three mounted officers that it became a question which would fall first. All three doubtless wanted to leave; but neither wished the other to know it, and neither wished first to suggest it.

Colonel Huger, however, broke the silence by remarking to Custer that he had often witnessed that kind of "taking the rebs in out of the wet," and if Custer could show nothing more that the party had better retire.

Just then an officer of the repulsed cavalry rode up, and on being asked by Custer why he did not "bring those men in," he replied, "General, I have not men enough." Custer then ordered reinforcements, and that brave line of Confederates were "taken in out of the wet."

After this Colonel Huger and Captain Brown dined with General Custer at his quarters. Custer told Huger that were it not for his success that evening he would be reprimanded by General Sheridan, as since ten o'clock in the morning he had orders to report at the head of the Sixth army corps; but seeing a wagon-train at that hour come into the Confederate column, and knowing it was out of its place, he determined to await his chance when it turned off, and make an attack.

"And now, gentlemen," said Custer, "if you will accompany me, I will give you a cavalry ride, as I will have to make a considerable detour to reach the head of the Sixth army corps."

Huger and Brown declining this invitation, they were escorted by a staff officer to the rear, the way being lighted by hundreds of burning wagons, for it was now nearly night.

Says Captain Brown: "A more genial gentleman in manners, a more dashing and gallant officer in the field, a more handsome and perfect physique in form and feature I never met than General Custer. I will never forget his long flowing ringlets of hair, and the perfect grace and ease with which he sat his beautiful horse on that ever memorable occasion."

Our captors generally were kind—even generous; for Sam Weisiger remembers that one noble fellow emptied the contents of a haversack into his hat, and the "hard tack" and bacon were heartily enjoyed by him and Doc Howard.

There was a roar of musketry all that afternoon. Lee's veterans were making their last heroic struggle, and many a Federal saddle was emptied of its rider; but by night there was a multitude of prisoners to sleep for the first time under the gleam of Federal bayonets.

In the morning General Custer made a sort of triumphal march around us. In the cavalcade were exhibited some dozen or more battle-torn Confederate flags, while a band of musicians played "Old Massa's Gone Away."

We were soon marched, under guard, rapidly in the direction of Petersburg. On the road, as we were passing a Boston battery, a youth cried out to Willie Evans, "Johnny, I'll give you a gold dollar for your pipe." Evans gladly made the exchange. Another one of these Boston boys gave Tom Alfriend a blanket.

Camping at night in the open field, we received rations, and of much better quality than we were used to; but, it may be truthfully added, the quantity was utterly inadequate. Individuals, as I have indicated, were very generous; but we were still doomed to suffer, not only from excessive fatigue, but hunger.

Before marching, in the morning, one of our men scratched up the soft earth under some bushes, and made a hole deep enough to lay himself in it, and we covered him over with loose dirt and leaves. The guard passed around the spot without noticing it, and he thus escaped several months of prison life.

It would be difficult to describe and impossible to exaggerate the hardships of the march to City Point. On the last day of the tramp we started from a point about fourteen miles from Petersburg, and when one set of guards broke down, we were halted only long enough for them to be relieved by fresh guards, and the rapid tramp was resumed. I say, rapid; for sometimes we were compelled to go at a double-quick. In going through a camp near Petersburg a kind-hearted Federal hastily gave Geo. Jones a handful of ground coffee, which he divided with me. I took it at one mouthful, and that was all the food I had that day.

In passing through Petersburg we found every window and door filled with the sad faces of the noble women, who wished to show their sympathy for us. One Federal said to Weisiger that he was glad we came through Petersburg, as otherwise they would never have seen the pretty faces of our ladies. They had persistently remained indoors since the Federal army occupied the town.

As, late in the day, we neared City Point, our tired and famished five thousand had straggled to that extent that the officer commanding had to order them to close up. This necessitated double-quicking, which, in our condition, was a terrible test of endurance. Some men dropped, as if dead, while making the effort to obey. At one time I felt as if nature was exhausted, and instinctively saying, " O God! " between my clinched teeth, I expected to fall too ; but opportunely a slower pace was allowed.

15

Arriving at City Point, a drunken officer came up to a cluster of our boys and ordered them to stand in due military order. This they did; and he told them to so remain until he returned. They would be there now if they had literally obeyed orders, for that was the last we saw of him.

Another officer came up to Willie Evans, doubtless noticing his extreme youthfulness, and said: "My boy, don't you want to go home? General Lee has surrendered, and, if you will take the oath, I can get you home." This offer Evans indignantly refused. Still the officer plead with him, all the kindness of his heart shown in his face; but Evans was "truly loyal," and would not desert his comrades.

At night it rained—a chilly April rain, that poured steadily upon our shelterless and starving boys. Day dawned, and still the heavens were dark with weeping clouds.

At the wharf lay the transport steamer *Neptune*, from which a herd of cattle had lately been unloaded. Into this ship the prisoners were marched. It was wet and filthy, having been but carelessly washed. Lucky those who happened to get on the deck, for there at least was fresh air. It was the fortune of a number of the Parker boys to get into the lower part of the ship. Here they were so crowded that there was scarcely standing room, and the only source of ventilation was a rough window. Soon the vessel dropped down the river, and we were on the way to prison.

Still no rations. There was no room in the filthy hole even for rest. When night came, I pillowed my head on George Jones' bosom, and tucked up my feet, rooster fashion, and went to sleep. Hundreds around me did likewise. I was awakened by loud cries and curses, such as, "D——n you, take your feet off my nose!" "Who in the h——l are you kicking!" The sleeping boys had forgotten their cramped quarters, and were stretching out quite recklessly. I raised up. The air was sickening—deathly. I quickly put my head to the floor. The night was damp and chilly, and the men near the window had closed it. I asked them to open it. They refused. It was a matter of life or death to me, and I said it should be opened. Just then I heard the words, "I'll go with you, Bob," and recognized the voice of George Fowlkes. It was difficult to reach the closed window without treading on some one's body and provoking a fight; but we got there and opened it, and stood guard over it the rest of the night. In the morning negro guards came around, with bayonets fixed, gruffly asking, "Got any dead here?" "Got any dead here?" Men had died among us during the night, and we did not know it.

Sam Weisiger had a more pleasant experience. Our guards were negroes, officered by white men. One of these sable sentinels stood near Sam's rude pillow. His gun was at "order arms," the barrel resting against his shoulder. He actually went to sleep, and Sam and one or two other boys slipped

the gun from his embrace, and hid it under blankets.
Then he was touched to awaken him, and of all
frightened men he was ludicrous to see. He begged
piteously for his gun; said if it was found out on
him he would be shot; and added, " Boss, if you'll
git my gun, I'll bring you a whole pot of nice coffee." The gun was returned, and Sam and his
friends got the coffee.

Rations were at last issued us, and in abundance;
but there was no system, and the shrewdest and
strongest were first supplied, to the neglect of the
weak. The famished prisoners pressed against the
place where the food was dispensed, and the negroes with their muskets at "charge bayonet," kept
saying, "Dress back dar!" "Dress back dar!"
Several of the prisoners thus received slight wounds.
My friend George Jones, who was lithe and strong,
climbed over the backs of the surging throng, and
brought me an abundance of crackers and bacon.
This I devoured ravenously, though the meat was
uncooked. As I had fasted for days, this gorging
with food was dangerous to health, if not life; but
I experienced no ill effect, except extreme thirst,
and for some time there was no water to be had.
We let down canteens into the bay, and drew up the
salt water; but of course could not drink it. After
much suffering, we were supplied with fresh water.

Point Lookout, in Maryland, was a great military
prison-city. A narrow strip of land, with the Chesapeake bay on one side, and the broad Potomac on

the other, it required only a small force of men to prevent the escape of the fifteen or twenty thousand prisoners who were there incarcerated. In April, 1865, General Barnes was in command, assisted by Major Brady.

Before entering the prison, our boys stood in line in front of Barnes' headquarters to be searched.

"Johnny," said one of the guards to Evans, "if you have any gold or silver, put it in your shoe."

This friendly advice was given none too soon; for Evans' gold dollar had hardly reached the bottom of his shoe when he felt a hand in his pocket from behind, and it was turned inside out. This gold dollar, the price of the pipe he sold the Boston boy, proved a little fortune to Evans in the prison.

This prison-city was enclosed by a high fence, on top of which was a grand walk for the sentinels, and on the inner side, a few feet from the fence, was a ditch, called the "dead line." The city was divided by twelve streets, running at right angles to the bay. On each street two rows of tents or cracker-box houses (built by ingenious prisoners) faced each other. Each street constituted a "division." On the side farthest from the bay, and at the end of the "division" streets, was a broad street called the "Parade." Across the "Parade," and fronting it, were the cook-houses. In each cook-house there were long tables, from which the prisoners were fed. There were a number of gates, and at certain times we were allowed free egress through those on the bay-side, and to walk on the beach or bathe, though bathing was not very popular on account of the defiled condition of the water, the "necessaries" being placed there. In the prison grounds were also a chapel, a sutler's store, and a small library.

In this great prison our boys were scattered promiscuously, for they had to go to the quarters assigned them. Willie Evans and Tom Alfriend became inmates of "Lee's Miserables," a rather historical shanty, having been built by Hon. A. M. Keiley and his friends when they were prisoners. It was constructed of pieces of cracker-boxes, with tent-cloth roof. This little house had five inmates when Evans and Alfriend were invited to join them. It was thus already crowded, but they were noble fellows, and treated the newcomers as brethren. They were Tom Howard, of Portsmouth; Tom and William Dunn, of Norfolk; J. V. A. Walker, of Selma, Alabama; and another whose name, but not his kindness, has faded from memory.

Sam Weisiger was an ideal "reb"—lazy, plucky, and lucky. His luck did not desert him at Point Lookout. He was invited to share the bunk of George W. Moore, a South Carolinian, who had been in prison several months, and had built a cracker-box mansion. Sam says of him: "I wish here to pay a tribute to his noble and generous hospitality. My heart goes out to him in a flood of tender memories."

Thus the boys were scattered here and there; but all were not so lucky as Evans and Weisiger, and had to sleep in tents and eat only prison rations.

"I say, Johnny, I'm afraid it will make it harder for you fellows," said a kind-hearted sentinel to me soon after our arrival at Point Lookout. He alluded to the assassination of President Lincoln, of which we had just heard. It really seemed that this sentinel's opinion was verified by the facts, for soon the white guards were relieved by blacks, and there were other indications of vindictiveness.

Each division was divided into companies. About 6 o'clock A. M. the company was formed in line, and marched to the cook-house. Filing down on either side of the long tables, each man was halted in front of a small piece of cooked meat. Prisoners were watched to see that one man did not get two pieces, which he might possibly do by leaving a gap between himself and the next man.

About 9 o'clock A. M. bread was brought to our quarters. It was nicely baked, but in quantity was about as much as could be bought for three cents in any bake-shop.

At 12 M. the company was again marched to the cook-house, and stood in line at the tables. This was to get a cup of soup. There were men there to see that no prisoner got two cups. One was lucky to get soup thick with beans.

Thus at six, nine, and twelve o'clock each day we received food, and the design seemed to be that the prisoners would save the meat until the bread was received, and reserve a portion of the bread to eat with the soup at twelve o'clock. The fact was, however (and I give my own as a specimen experi-

ence), that in the morning I eat the small piece of
pork allowed at a few mouthfuls; also the bread as
soon as received, and then the soup—each separately.
Thus from noon until sunrise I had nothing to eat,
and I frequently went to my tent at night so weak
from hunger I could scarcely stand.

I forgot to mention cod-fish in this bill of fare,
which was issued in the afternoon—raw and salty.
Shaking the salt from it, and impelled by hunger,
we could eat but little of such food, even had it been
plentiful, without producing an unhealthy thirst.

There were a number of pumps on the grounds;
but the water they afforded was very brackish. We
called it "copperas water." It was unpleasant to
the taste, and caused a great deal of sickness. There
was only one pump that gave pure water, and that
was guarded. Access to it required a pass from
Colonel Brady, written with black ink, countersigned
with red. Henry Byrd, of Petersburg, had one, but
the red ink was blood. It is hardly necessary to say
that Brady had never seen it, although it bore a
clever imitation of his signature. Thus the twenty
thousand men had to drink the "copperas water" or
none.

Fortunately, the season was mild, and we did not
suffer from cold; but old prisoners told us that in
the bitter winter nights men actually froze to death
in their tents. One blanket only was allowed; if a
prisoner had two, one was taken from him.

As the spring advanced, and the weather became
mild, we availed ourselves of the privilege of bathing

in the bay, despite the defiling "necessaries" contiguous. Wooden posts marked the limits of our seaward range. If a bather went beyond them he was liable to be shot. I have stood many a time on one of these posts—a fair mark for a sentinel—and playfully debated with my comrades whether I should jump seaward or landward.

It was reported that a bather had been eaten by a shark, and next day the water was severely let alone. Some of us, who did not believe the shark story, went into the water as usual. One of our boys dived, and, coming up under another swimmer, clasped him with his hands, and badly frightened him.

If any disorder prevailed among the prisoners at night, the guards fired indiscriminately among them. Thus the innocent were as likely to suffer as the guilty.

No one who has never formed the "tobacco habit" can appreciate the sufferings of one who has been used to "the weed" and is deprived of it. Of course there was a great deal of suffering of this sort. Old quids were rarely seen on the streets of Lookout City. Disgusting as the fact may be, there were people who picked them up and used them. A wretched prisoner one day asked a negro sentinel to give him a chew of tobacco. The negro told him to come and get it. In order to do this the prisoner crossed the "dead line," when the sentinel shot him dead.

We were allowed to write to our friends, a half-sheet of note-paper being the limit; but that was read, and sometimes returned, by a Federal officer if the contents did not meet his approval. Condensed milk, mixed with a little water, was used to write between the lines. It did not show enough, after it was dry, to attract attention; but, when the paper was held to the fire, the writing between the lines became quite legible.

Happy was the prisoner who obtained a remittance from friends or relatives. It first came to Colonel Brady, who would send for him, give him the letter advising of the money being sent, and hand him a pass-book giving credit at the sutler's for the amount; but he never saw the money. You may be sure that the sutler was sufficiently considerate of the prisoner's health not to give him too much for his money.

Having nothing whatever to do, except to eat and sleep (and the eating required very little time), the men resorted to everything possible to relieve the monotony of prison life. The making of gutta-percha rings and other trinkets was a popular industry, as they could be readily sold to visitors who came to see the "terrible" Southerners. A man in the Seventh division made several hundred dollars in this way.

Storekeeping was common. Stock in trade varied from a chew of tobacco up to a barrel of flour. In fact, the science of political economy, at least in some degree, was illustrated in this prison-city. All came there poor, but a few months' residence made surprising changes. The shrewd and industrious became comparatively rich. There were "merchants," it was said, who dated their first step towards wealth from a shrewd trade with a chew of tobacco. A big-mouthed, loud-voiced fellow, in a tent near us, annoyed me much by his vociferous mode of advertising his business. He would lay on his back and bawl, "Here's your tobacco for your bread!" And if no one responded to this offer, he would next cry, "Here's your bread for your tobacco!" He looked very lazy, and evidently hoped to grow rich on somebody else's labor.

There were those who honestly went to work to improve their condition. A few pounds of flour, a pound of fat bacon, and a few sticks of wood was nearly all the material necessary to start a bakery. The result was a half-dozen hot cakes on a board at the tent-door, awaiting the man with "stamps," the most common currency. To this might be added tobacco, purchased from the sutler, and cut up into small pieces or "chews." These "chews" were also used as currency.

This display was often too tempting for the appetite and honesty of "the poor." One might occasionally see a man rush up to one of these stores, grab what he could in passing, and dart in among the tents with his stolen plunder. Then the cry, "Stop thief!" would be raised, and everybody would try to head him off. Often he would escape; but, if caught, he was taken to one of the barrels which served for the natural wants of the prisoners (we were not allowed to defile the camp) and soused head foremost in the water. He was then allowed to go, and seldom or never again infringed the code of honesty. Something like this was necessary to protect the "rights of property."

Newspapers were rarely or never seen. It was now two months since the surrender of Lee, and all the Confederate armies had disbanded. Why did the Government retain us in prison? Even intelligent men among us suggested that death or expatriation might be our fate. All sorts of rumors were afloat. Sometimes for amusement one man would say to another, " I heard that Brady said," etc., and in a few minutes fifty to a hundred men would gather around him. This sort of talk got the name of "grape," and an idle or incredible rumor was dismissed with the remark, " Oh, that's grape ! "

Of course, everybody was willing to "take the oath." A negro Confederate soldier, strange to say, was a solitary exception to the rule. He was the only dark-skinned "reb" whom I saw there. He was unreconstructed and "unreconstructible" the last time I saw him.

June came, and still no release. The sun glared against the whitewashed fences and the white tents. No trees were within the enclosure to tell us by their green leaves that summer had come. Only the black earth, the sickening water, and coarse, scant fare; and every way we looked, except skyward and seaward, was the monotonous, blinding white. Some men were thus temporarily blinded. The ships on the bay, with their white sails flapping in the wind, would arrest our attention for a while, and awaken thoughts of home and freedom, and then disappear.

It was under such influences that Andrew Nelson died—a gentle-hearted boy, who had been but a few weeks in the army when he was captured. He died from home-sickness, thinking of the loving mother and sisters far, far from his wretched pallet.

It was then, too, that Willie Evans sickened and almost died; but the boys rallied around him in his distress, and he lives now to say, "Noble and brave comrades, God bless you!"

Another kindly deed is remembered. Tom Todd was not captured, but he sent Robert Dunaway ten dollars when money was very scarce in Richmond. On him Dunaway lives to invoke, from his Ohio home, a heartfelt "God bless you!"

One night there was a storm—welcome storm! It broke the monotony of our dreary life. The waves dashed against the shore with a thundering sound, and the wind whistled wild music among the tents. Anything—anything but the dead calm of the prison-city!

At last, about the middle of June, we were allowed to take the oath of allegiance to the United States. Late one afternoon we were put aboard a steamer bound for Richmond, and night found us moving rapidly down the Chesapeake bay. The spray from the prow of the boat sprinkled the forward deck, but a number of the Parker boys lay there, and listened to the dashing water, and enjoyed the cooling wind.

What if the cause was lost? All was not lost. We had youth and health and hope, and when the morning sun glanced back from the green shores of the James, how soothing to our eyes was the emerald hue, and how pleasant the light that bathed the distant landscape!

"Onward!" whispered the good angel of Hope. "Onward to new fields of nobler strife, of which the bloody past are but the symbols, and where the right never fails!"

CHAPTER XIII.

A BACKWARD GLANCE.

"Your remembrance is all the more gratifying to me, because my separation during the last year of the war from the Army of Northern Virginia would render natural a forgetfulness of me by my old comrades, whose joys and dangers I shared through the earlier campaigns of that army."—*Gen. Delaware Kemper.*

WHO among the battalion veterans can have forgotten John Donnell Smith, lieutenant, then captain, of Battery "A"? When our twenty-six guns deployed for action, who so cool and statue-like, as he stood, looking through spectacles, with his arms folded as if at "parade rest"? A glance at him was enough to calm the nervous, and make us feel that there were cool heads among us as well as ready hands.

See how pleasantly that gallant Marylander writes about the boy battery and the battalion as he knew them more than twenty years ago:

"In July, 1862, five mounted batteries were encamped in a woods skirting an old field on the Williamsburg road, a few miles east of Richmond. They were temporarily united under the command of Major Delaware Kemper, and a regimental court-martial had been appointed by him to meet at Captain Parker's quarters. As members of that court an acquaintance was then made which events, not at the time foreseen, converted into a close comradeship in arms, continuous thenceforth up to the Appomattox surrender, and into a friendship not less continuous, and even more lasting.

"As we seated ourselves at a table under a fly in front of his wall-tent, there was in view a pretty scene of alligned guns and caissons, picketed horses, harness on racks, tents in files, and grounds neatly policed. The company had but recently been mustered into service, and I remember accounting in that way for a stricter conformance with army regulations, in the style of its park and encampment, than prevailed in companies that had been longer in the field. But it must be admitted that Parker never fell into those careless, slip-shod ways, for which so many of us found an excuse in the exigencies of actual service.

"This assemblage of batteries illustrated an important change at that time taking place in artillery organization. The evils of brigade batteries had been recently experienced. The delay in massing an adequate number of guns, and the futile employment of an inadequate number, had been exhibited respectively at White Oak Swamp and Malvern Hill. Division battalions were now forming under division chiefs. But it was not until after the Maryland campaign that such organizations were regarded as permanent, and were regularly equipped with field and staff.

"The tactical advantages of the battalion were soon to have their finest illustration in the handling of our own guns. Jordan's, Rhett's, Parker's, and Eubank's batteries, commanded by Colonel S. D. Lee, with Kemper as Major, were posted in the centre of our line at Manassas on the afternoon of 30th August. The enemy, having massed his troops in front of our left (held by Jackson), had pushed forward his first line until it became engaged at close quarters in a fierce and bloody struggle. It was at this critical moment, when a second and third line of great strength moved up to support the first, that Colonel Lee, with the true instinct and rapid decision of the born soldier, advanced his eighteen guns to easy range, changed front, and concentrated their fire upon the exposed flank of the supporting columns. I state the situation substantially in the language of the report of the Commanding General, and add the comment of President Davis: 'I have reason to believe that at the last great conflict on the field of Manassas he [Lee] served to turn the tide of battle and consummate the victory.'

"Colonel Lee was steadily at work, improving the discipline and instruction of his command, when I joined in October at Winchester upon the consolidation of Page's with Jordan's company. Battery drills were frequent, and even battalion manœuvres occasionally attempted. Twenty-six guns changing front made an imposing spectacle. Nor could better grounds have been desired than those wide-rolling fields around Winchester—once so lovely in their

16

luxuriant crops—then untilled, unfenced, and trodden bare by hostile armies in quickly alternating possession.

"A generous solicitude was exhibited by Colonel Lee in the matter of his successor. It was understood that by his influence Lieutenant-Colonel Alexander was induced to devote himself to a different arm of the service from that to which he had been attached in the United States as well as in the Confederate States army. In the former he had served as an officer of high promise in the Engineer Corps; in the latter he was holding the positions of Chief of Ordnance and Chief of the Signal Corps on the staff of the Commanding General. His true vocation might have been missed throughout the war, and his best services lost to the country, had he not been prevailed upon at this time to take the command of troops. He was our Colonel from November, 1862, to February, 1864; and afterwards our Brigadier-General and Chief of Artillery for the First Corps.

"A technical acquaintance with all the minutiæ of the complex *matériel* of artillery was united in General Alexander with the finest comprehension of the principles of its employment. His enthusiastic faith in the arm was an education for officers serving under him,—chiefly soldiers of the occasion, more familiar with the civil professions than with that of arms. They have not forgotten the sympathy and support he gave to every effort in the performance of duty.

" The happy fortune of the battalion in its field-officers continued throughout the war. Lieutenant-Colonel Huger, of South Carolina, an *élève* of the West Point Academy, who had resigned from the United States army, had been for the preceding year second in command, and succeeded Alexander. Jordan, to our great satisfaction, remained with us as Major. He was an artillerist of experience, of the soundest judgment, and full of resource under difficulties.

" Reminiscences of those years would be incomplete indeed without mention of our horses. Where-ever responsibility existed for the efficiency of a gun, there dwelt unceasing anxiety about the condition of its teams. If it could not keep up on the march, or execute an ordered movement, what was its use, and why should not its officers, cannoneers, and drivers be carrying instead a score or more of muskets? The care of horses under adverse conditions, what a chapter could be written on that topic! His own shortcomings in duty, more keenly felt afterwards than at the time, would take up a large part of such a chapter. How urgently he would insist upon the wisdom of those forms and methods that are but the expression of wide experience. An almost despotic authority existed for enforcing compliance, but through indolence or weak good-nature he tolerated their neglect. Honestly reviewing the whole subject, he would admit that a close personal supervision, verifying for every hour of day and night that each particular horse was faring as well as circumstances made possible, would have reduced by a large percentage the number of animals he turned in as unserviceable. The adverse conditions, which he could not alter, were irregular or short issues of forage, distressful marchings with an infantry column, and service at hazardous positions not permitting the removal of harness. But the mischief came largely from the following causes, which were more or less within his control: careless picketing; exposure to weather with too much restraint of movement; feeding on the ground; neglect of make-shift substitutes for long-forage; clandestine loading of blankets, rubber-cloths and tent-pieces under drivers- and valise-saddles; keeping teams with guns where the risk might have been assumed of dismounting chests and sending limbers and caissons to the rear. These sentences will recall sad scenes of poor, trembling beasts with tails frozen between their legs, loins coated with snow, pasterns cracked with scratches, raw withers, gnawing at everything within reach except their untouched corn, or in summer-time succumbing in weakness to devouring swarms of flies. The Confederate's slumbers are still visited by bad dreams of the rottenness of those bottom-lands, soaked, not drained, by the hundred tributaries of the North Anna, Mattapony, and Rapidan; of teams balking midway in the winter-swollen floods of the Holston; of carriages dissected and transported piece-meal; of men in the mud tugging at drag-ropes and prolonges.

"But brighter scenes are not forgotten, when

guns danced gaily over the roughest roads, and nothing was an obstacle; when Woolfolk, under the eyes of Jackson, advanced firing by half-battery on the Plank road; when Jordan, quartering a 20°-grade, climbed the Fairview Heights and unlimbered on the glacis of the breastworks just abandoned by the enemy; when Parker flew from hill to hill, pounding away at Burnside in full retreat on Knoxville; when Fickling, without orders, and giving the lead to the battery behind him, dashed through the breastworks at Foster's Farm into the open field, and eight guns right-wheeled into battery, delivering their fire across Pickett's front upon the attack at Cold Harbor. The Texas brigade was being hurried by to the threatened point, but found time to cheer at the sight of those figures standing out against the evening sky.

"A finer sight still was that of the whole twenty-six guns deploying, and forwarding into battery on Strawberry Plains. But grandest of all artillery manœuvres was that of the battalion, with a front of over four hundred yards, sweeping at a gallop down the long slope at Gettysburg, every man of the six hundred yelling like a madman. Dearing, whose command was not up, was riding about looking for a job, and saw us coming from afar. With energy of speech and gesture, he ordered a long line of prisoners, crouched along a fence, to pull it down. It seemed in an instant to be picked up and laid flat, and there was no check to the rush. The line spread out to the right and left in search of positions, and halted as they were found. These were chiefly in a peach orchard. In the smoke we were soon lost to each other's view, and each section fought according to its own lights, which were none of the best.

"Jordan's right section was beginning to suffer, when Dearing, who by this time had somehow lost his cap, shouted, 'They've got your range! I'll show you a better place!' and led the way out of the orchard by the left, and then down a lane, with the section trotting along after him. Wounded men fluttered out of the way of the horses and wheels like crippled birds, looking up with imploring eyes. One of them, in a sort of Zouave uniform, raised himself half way, shouting and waving for 'the star-spangled banner.'

"There was no going far in that direction, and the better place turned out to be where Barksdale's Mississippi brigade was slowly yielding ground, in good order and firing. That bareheaded volunteer disappeared in the smoke, doubtless bent on getting some one else into trouble.

"It was a hot, sultry evening, and the clouds of smoke settled everywhere. The flash of the enemy's guns, followed instantly by their report, was the only clue to their position. That would have been an ever-vanishing target. It was thought best to search the front with canister and with a low fire of one-second shell, in the hope that they might have the luck of meeting with something; for of case-shot there was none, and never was, unless it had been captured. Evening shades began to be added. Those

Mississippi friends were no longer about. Unknown voices had called out warnings; and now Woolfolk came clattering past with his twenty-pounders, and shouted, 'You'd better get out of that!' Replacing a shattered gun-limber with one from a caisson that had lost half its horses, the cannoneers mounted the chests with wounded comrades in their arms, and the section galloped back to the peach trees. After dark a sergeant was sent with teams, and hauled off the parts of carriages and the harness that had been left behind.

"There were some droll characters in Battery A, but a pencil rather than words would be needed to depict them. Nothing was so sure to provoke the often remarked "levity" of the Southern soldier as the figure on the march of our wheezy bugler, Pitzenberger—'old Pitz,' better known to the First corps than many of its generals. A more serious, but hardly less quaint personage was Meloth, the silent one of the German contingent, the old Algerian soldier, as melancholy of aspect as though he were ever thinking of 'Bingen, sweet Bingen on the Rhine.' I could never make out that he had the slightest idea of what the war was about; but he was as true to the flag as if he had known by heart the whole constitutional argument. When, at Appomattox, a parole was handed to Meloth, he took from his belt a mass of Confederate notes (savings from his pay!) and asked what he must do about it. I felt as if I had been passing forged paper. A captured Irishman was once overheard remonstrating with his country-

man, Tim Hogan, 'What he had to do with it all.'
Tim confined his line of argument to the view that
the cause of the South was just like that of Ireland,
and he was fighting against 'oppression.'

"At Sailor's Creek, our last battlefield, Sergeant
Reed,*—who had lost an arm at Sharpsburg, but
had returned to duty in the field,—distinguished
himself by his energy in getting into action a re-
captured gun. His brother Thomas rammed, Henry
Huddleston and Strasser served as reduced numbers,
and the ever reliable Corporal Parker pointed the last
shot ever fired by the battalion. It set fire to a barn
occupied by the enemy's skirmishers. I have often
wondered how young Reed stood up to his work that
day. A paroxysm of fever and ague was on him at
the time. When, a few days later, we took position
near Appomattox Court-house, Sergeant Reed asked
where the sick men, including his brother, should be
put. I pointed to a clump of trees just in front of
the unlimbered guns. He looked as if he thought
I had lost my senses. General Alexander had just
whispered to me that the Army of Northern Virginia was about to surrender."

JOE AND HIS FAMILY.

There was attached to our battery a sort of me-
nagerie, consisting of a cow, several hens, and one
rooster, all under the charge of Joe, the Captain's
body servant. Besides being the guardian of this

* Rev. J. C. Reed, pastor of Trinity church, Richmond, Va.

family, Joe was hostler, cook, washer and ironer, milker, and caterer for the Captain's table. He had also charge of the ambulance, which General Lee had allowed our battery as a special favor, as our Captain rendered medical service to his own men. In this ambulance were carried a large medicine-chest, camp stools and bed, table crockery, surgical instruments, tent and fly, stores, etc.; also, the hens and rooster; and last, not least, two violins and a guitar.

It required a nice adjustment of forces to so arrange the varied contents of this wagon as to protect the lighter from contact with the heavier articles. The roads were often very rough; much marching was done at night, and ruts and rocks could not be avoided. Sometimes the hens and rooster would make a loud noise, showing that they had not been able to maintain their ground against the heavy medicine-chest, and a halt was called to investigate the complaint. Sometimes the medical instruments would get uncomfortably jammed, and had to be protected. So soon as a halt was made for the night, the fowls were taken out, the hens liberated, but the rooster tied to a wheel-spoke by his "hind leg." The hens, true to the instincts of the female sex, were faithful to their lord, and never wandered far from the wagon.

It is customary in ordinary marches for the battalion commander to send forward, some time before night, an officer to select a camp-ground. In summer the officer selects open ground, near a branch;

but in winter he prefers a southern hill-side, near a
forest, where shelter from the cold wind is secured.
But in forced marches it often happens that a halt
is called long after dark, and no preparation is made
for a camping ground. Under such circumstances,
the first thing done after the horses are unhitched is
to find water. Joe was generally the first to start.
Taking his two buckets, with the rattling dipper, he
might be seen striding down grade. It was singular
how quickly he found it. The reader may be puzzled to know how he could tell where to go for
water in the thick darkness of the night; but both
reason and (I suppose) instinct told him he must
seek some low place, and thitherward he bent his
steps, soon to return with two full buckets. No one
asked if the water was clear or good. It had to be
drunk anyhow, and these were unnecessary questions.
By the way, the boys used to steal Joe's water, and
he found it necessary to hide it; but in spite of all
his precautions, many a sly dipperful was obtained.
He was thus careful because the company usually
broke camp at daybreak, and the Captain must have
an early breakfast.

As the war progressed and our horses got poor,
Joe found it necessary to bring the cow into requisi-
tion as a beast of burden. She was saddled; tin
pans, frying-pans, coffee pot, etc., were hung upon
the saddle, and the docile brute moved on utterly
oblivious of the clatter on her back. Soldiers made
merry of the cow and her pack; but she moved along
the road, with thousands of infantry crowding her,

only asking to be let alone. She was usually tied to a caisson, but often she was turned loose, and followed the battery as if she was an enlisted soldier. She travelled hundreds of miles, if not thousands.

This cow enabled the Captain to "live well," in the eyes of the soldiers. He could have rice pudding, that is, before the sugar gave out. He could also have buttermilk, sugar or no sugar. Buttermilk to a soldier is nectar. Joe would, before the march began, fill the Captain's big Yankee canteen with fresh milk, and in summer time, by twelve o'clock, the jogging along on horseback would convert the sweet into butter milk, and by dipping the canteen into water occasionally—covered, as it was, with thick woolen cloth, and dangling in the air— the buttermilk was soon very cool and very delicious. In taking a drink from this canteen the Captain had to close his lips well over the mouth of it, lest the soldiers should see milk on his moustache, and it would be impossible to refuse a fellow a "drink." Every one could get water on the march, as every one had a canteen; so that the Captain was not often called upon for the use of his canteen.

During the last winter of the war Joe had an addition to his family, in the shape of a large, raw-boned brindle cow, which strayed into our camp, and as there was but one other cow in camp, this new recruit soon sought fellowship with her. No one calling for this new cow, Joe thought by dividing his little provender he might get more milk, and he soon began to think himself owner of the brindle cow, and she was regularly milked. At first she was wild and ungovernable, but soon, with the good example of the old veteran cow, she became used to camp life.

It so happened that on the 2d of April, 1865, Joe was in Richmond, and had ridden the Captain's best horse. Unlike most soldiers, Joe seemed to prefer camp life to the pleasures of home, although he had but lately married; but the Captain insisted that he should visit his family in Richmond as often as was convenient. His absence, however, on that particular 2d of April might have been fortunate for him, but not for his master. That afternoon news came of the break in the lines at Petersburg. We must prepare to fall back that night. The Captain, after sending off his wife in the ambulance to Richmond with a family servant, next considered how to carry his baggage. Joe was gone; also ambulance and riding-horse. Happily, he bethought him of the new brindle, and of the old war-horse (cow). So, after killing the rooster and hens with sticks and rocks, a little bow-legged fellow named Carlton was ordered to "saddle the cows." The old cow was quickly loaded with the chickens and other rations, as well as the Captain's baggage; and Carlton then proceeded to put the stew-pan, coffee-pot, skillet, and other cooking utensils upon the brindle. But it was soon found necessary to "make her fast" to a pine tree to secure dispatch in loading her. It was now almost dark, and the battery was about to move, and the Captain, learning that everything was ready, told Carlton to "let go the lines," and make the brindle follow in the wake of the old cow, that had just commenced the line of march in the best order. But, alas! no sooner had the ropes slipped off the brindle's horns than, with head, heels, and tail high in the air, she sped down the hill, the sound of her bellowing commingling with the clatter of tin cups, pans, and skillet, forming a base and tenor never before heard on earth.

Although those who witnessed this sight were sad almost unto death, they found it impossible not to laugh. The Captain had to lean against a tree for support. After freeing herself from every vestige of her pack, the brindle slowly returned, seeking her companion the veteran cow. The scattered load was soon collected and again packed securely on the brindle's back; but no sooner were the lines let go than, with a bound and a terrific bellow, she fled down the hill, this time never to return.

Joe had another office: he was a watch-keeper. Before going into battle it was common for the men and officers who had watches to hand them over to Joe, who was sure to keep well to the rear. The reader may not know that the first thing sought for on the dead soldier's body was his watch. Joe took great pride in guarding well his treasures, though no compensation was made him for his services.

The boys had quite a number of jokes on Joe. He was not a soldier, and he knew it. He was helping to fight, and he helped manfully; but shooting, or being shot at, was not his plan or purpose.

On one occasion, while driving quietly along the road, no one dreaming of an enemy near, sudden as lightning a solid cannon-ball took off the head of one of Joe's horses; and it never has been determined in how short a time Joe got the dead horse out and and a live horse in the harness. Of course the Captain's attention was instantly turned towards the direction from whence came the shot, but it was but a minute before he looked behind to see how Joe was getting on in extricating the dead horse, when, lo! the ambulance, with two live horses, was seen in the distance at a full gallop!

On another occasion, we had spent the night near the enemy, and the cannonading was quite heavy early in the morning, but there was no danger to us unless the enemy changed his fire. It was noticed that Joe had the fidgets, and was clumsy with his dough and skillet, but after a while the inevitable short-cake and coffee was on the camp-chest, and the Captain proceeded to eat his breakfast. Having finished, he said, "Joe, eat your breakfast, and hitch up and go to the rear." Encircling plates, cups, coffee-pot, and everything else on the table-cloth with his long arms, he replied, "My God, Mars' William, this no place to eat breakfas'!" And he soon found his way to the rear.

The picture of this faithful servant will never be effaced from the memory of any man in the battery. He was six feet in his stockings, with short body but long arms and legs, and active as a cat. His high cheek bones and color made him resemble a Seminole Indian. His countenance was grave, and not often lighted by a smile, except when, after the toils of the day, he solaced himself with a pipe of good tobacco.

Joe is now, and has been for many years, sexton of Trinity church, Richmond ; and a Christmas never comes that he does not send his former master a fat turkey, with the " fixings," often saying to Major Parker's wife, " Miss Ellen, me and Mars' William, in de war, was jest like brothers."

CHAPTER XIV.

AFTER TWENTY YEARS.

"The past is not : the hues in which 'tis drest
　　Fond memory supplies.
The future is not : hope-born, within the breast,
　　Its fancied joys arise.
The present is not : like the lightning's gleam,
　　Its brief illusions seem.
This is the life allotted unto man :
A hope, a memory, a fleeting moment's span."

TWENTY years ! That seems a long time. The fifth of a century ! That seems longer still. Twenty years since the curtain fell upon the bloody drama in which two million men strove for mastery on the American continent !

It is "decoration day" in America's great metropolis. Stand with me on Broadway, where the grand street is faced by Union Square, with its flowers and trees and springing fountain. Here Washington and Lincoln are equally honored—the one as the founder of the infant republic, the other as the saviour of a great nation. Flowers bedeck the equestrian statue of one, and flowers almost hide the form of him who said, "With charity for all, and with malice toward none, we will maintain the right, as we understand the right."

The great city is in holiday attire this beautiful

30th day of May, sacred to the patriot dead of the
Union. That matchless spire of Grace-church points
to a cloudless sky, and gentle winds are caressing
the flags that float from a hundred staves. Though
it is yet early in the day, soldiers in red and soldiers
in gray are seen going hither and thither, and the
air is full of the busy hum of preparation.

As the sun climbs the heavens towards noon the
grand street is lined by throngs of expectant people,
and the doors and windows of all the houses are
filled with eager men, women, and children. The
national colors are waving from ten thousand hands,
and the roar of a hundred drums announces that the
procession is coming!

How grandly they march! How brightly gleam
the thousands of bayonets! How proudly yonder
color-bearer holds aloft the national banner, while
the soft May breeze toys with its glittering folds,
and the sunlight blazes in glory from each silken
star!

See that grand-looking officer, with his mounted
staff. His horse steps proudly to the music, as if
conscious of the noble burden he bears.

"Who is he?" asks Robert Cannon, for the
"rebel" boy of twenty years ago is looking with
delighted eyes upon all this "pomp and circumstance" of military show.

"That's Hancock," is the reply of a polite New
Yorker.

Instantly Robert Cannon's hands are clapping in
applause, and thousands join him, while other thou-

17

sands wave tiny flags and handkerchiefs in honor of the hero of Gettysburg.

Regiment after regiment and brigade after brigade marches past. There is the far-famed and fastidious "Seventh," and when Cannon sees it his memory recalls a scene of his boyhood when that regiment was the guest of his own "First Virginia," and how Richmond people almost wept when the New Yorkers embarked on a steamship, while the crowd on shore sang "Auld Lang Syne."

There goes the "gallant Sixty-ninth," which one of its own members has toasted as "equal to none," but which all who saw it in war would pronounce equal to any. There are also fat Germans on horses, who remind one of those who fought "mit Siegel," but who look too heavy to have ever followed that leader in his more rapid movements!

The bands are playing their most inspiring strains. Hark! what tune is that? It is "Marching Through Georgia," and the blood of the Southerner rebels against the humiliation of a great State thus perpetuated in a song.

Let us now repair to Greenwood—that Eden of the dead. Let us pass under the sculptured story of the resurrection that arches its entrance, and ascend the hill which is crowned by Battle Monument. Standing there, the eye takes in at a glance the two great cities whose denizens come here at last to find their long home. The waters of New York bay are flashing in the sunlight, with the dim outline of the Staten hills and the Jersey shore rimming the picture.

See this monument. It is erected by the city of
New York in honor of the mighty army she sent
forth to battle for the Union cause; but few of
the dead are sleeping here. The soil of Greenwood
is too precious to inter the bones of the humble men
whom merchant princes paid to pour out their life-
blood on the altar of "liberty and union." Far
away, under Southern suns, the grass is kept green
on their graves, and the winds through the Southern
pines sigh mournfully their requiem.

It is "memorial day" in Richmond. In the afternoon a regiment of infantry marches to Hollywood,
where a simple pile of rough granite marks the
ground where thousands of Confederates are buried.
Thither have already repaired women and children
carrying flowers, and each grave receives its tribute
of these emblems of affection.

Following the infantry, few of whom have ever
seen service in war, comes a veteran association of
Union soldiers, commanded by a man whose empty
sleeve tells his history. Next come the Confederate
veterans, many of whom bear marks of hard-fought
fields. The little procession halts near a newly-made
grave under the shadow of the granite monument.
A Union veteran steps forward and places on the
grave an elaborate floral decoration. Hundreds of
smaller tributes are then showered upon it, and Federal and Confederate vie with each other in honoring
the memory of Pickett, the Southern hero of Gettysburg. Prayer is offered, words of tender eulogy

are spoken, and then, lighted by the rays of the setting sun, the visitors slowly depart. Such is our American "war of the roses," thank God!"

Not Greenwood, with all its wealth of art and help of nature, can surpass, if it equals, this Richmond "city of the dead." Surely here, if anywhere on earth, is rest—"rest for the weary soul." Let us walk along this quiet road in the subdued light of the evening. The roar of the river, tumbling over a thousand huge rocks, breaks against the hill where Monroe is entombed, and falls in soothing requiem in this lowly vale where we are walking. Yonder brook flows softly, as if fearing to disturb the holy silence; and the trees on its banks cast a tender gloom over the sleepers at their feet. On yonder hill-side a thousand evergreens and flowers are clinging in mournful sympathy to shafts that rise white in the thickening shadows.

Here are the bones of Presidents—Virginia's Tyler and Monroe. Here are the tombs of soldiers, whose swords flashed defiance in the face of Virginia's foes—her Hill, her Stuart, and her Pegram. And here, more than all, are the "unknown and unrecorded dead"—those who did not even expect that their names would be remembered, but were content to march, fight, starve, or die in defence of their country's honor.

The river is roaring its eternal lullaby. The moon shimmers its silvery radiance through the trees, among which the evening breeze is whispering an unwritten story. It is night, always solemn, but

grandly solemn among these trees, stretching out
their long arms over tombstones. Here is the grave
of another hero. What is that, rising white and
ghostly, above it? Do not be startled. It is not a
sword, but a cross.

Twenty years! And the survivors of the boy
company are scattered from Virginia to California,
and from Ohio to Louisiana. A few of them, however, are gathered in reunion on one of the old
battle-grounds. The roll is called, but for many
names the response is given, "Dead." Here, however, is Weisiger, from Georgia, and Tucker, from
Pennsylvania; and California sends us back our one-
armed lieutenant, Stafford Parker. Here also is
Henry Atkinson, who left us for the cavalry, but
served his State gallantly, and was twice wounded.
We miss our one-armed bugler Kavanaugh; but
Charlie Cowardin, the prince of good fellows, blows
lustily a cornet, while the "old boys," with Captain
Brown at their head, make the wildwoods ring with
"*Vive la Compagnie!*"

Letters are read from Generals Kemper, Lee,
Alexander, and Huger; and then Major Parker,
now gray in years, if not in dress, but with the old
fire in his eyes and the old stern emphasis in his
tone, says:

"We meet to-day, fellow-soldiers, after twenty
years' separation, with mingled feelings of pleasure
and pain. Our sad farewell at Appomattox, and
the subsequent struggle of long, weary years to re-

pair our fortunes, bring up a thousand memories—
some bright, but many dark and gloomy. But we
meet to-day specially to renew our friendship, which
twenty years have not, I am sure, broken or weakened. We all, while we clasp hands, thank God
and take courage. If we did our duty, it matters
not how the struggle ended. We are not responsible.

"While war is a great scourge, it is not without
its blessings. It is a great school for courage, self-
possession, endurance, patience, obedience to orders,
and contentment. But it is in this high school especially that grand and glorious patriotism is fostered
and developed. In a conversation with my father,
several years before the late war, I said it was
doubtful whether 'patriotism' was anything more
than a sentiment, and partook often of an illiberal
party spirit, finding its expression or power sometimes in selfishness. But I had not then felt its
spell.

"Patriotism is of Heaven. It is a universal instinct, extending through all the animal kingdom
from the ant up to man, and is strongest in the
most enlightened. It has love for its foundation—
love of home, love of friends and neighbors, love of
trees and running brooks, of rivers, valleys, and
mountains, and of the graves of our ancestors. It
is love the highest, deepest, strongest, most noble,
and unselfish. It is to love "sweet home," next
only to the heavenly home. For both how cheerfully has many a noble man surrendered his life-

blood, and was glad that he was counted worthy to pay the price!

"Will not the 'three hundred' live forever! Was it in vain they died? What was their short and humble lives worth to them and to the world? But dying, they have been a lesson to a hundred generations, and Sparta will be honored as long as one brave heart survives. Those gallant fellows who fell by our side on the field have not lived nor died in vain. They are in the true line of succession of noble men of every land and nation. They are akin to all the bright and noble spirits that the world has embalmed in song and story. Sleep on, brave comrades! May a glorious resurrection await you!"

INDEX

INDEX TO UPDATED EDITION BY ROBERT K. KRICK

Brown, David A., 80, 104–7, 183
Brown, J. Thompson, 27, 37, 41–42,
    45, 106, 115–25, 128, 142,
    148–49, 161, 199, 217, 221–22,
    261; photo, frontispiece; quoted,
    46, 93, 145, 223
Bryant, Robert A., 44
Burnside, Ambrose E., 73, 77, 127,
    245
Burwell (civilian near Millwood), 137
Butler, Benjamin F., 205, 212
Byrd, Henry, 232

Cabell, Henry C., 126
Camp Lee, Va., 19–21
Campbell Station, battle of, 162, 167
Cannon, Robert (pseudonym), viii
Carlton, George W., 252–53
Carmel Church, Va., 96–114
Caroline County, Va., 43, 96–114
Carroll, Charles, 18
Castle Booker, 108
Castle Thunder, 106
Catholic nuns, 40, 42–43
cavalry performance, 72
Cavnaugh, John, 261
Chancellorsville, battle of, 115–36,
    146, 219, 245
Chattanooga, Tenn., 155–61, 169, 219
Chesterfield Court-house, Va., 216
Chickamauga, battle of, 155, 161
Christian (pseudonym), 17–18
City Point, Va., 225–27
Clark, Gibson, 138, 143, 162
Clarke, Robert N., 40–41

Clopton, William I., 125
Cobb, Thomas R. R., 81–82
Cogbill, John A., 42, 92, 128, 161
Cogbill, William B., 27, 42, 92,
    119–21, 143–44, 150, 161–62
Cold Harbor, battle of, 204, 245
Colston, Frederick M., 146
Condrey, Madison E., 161–62
conscripts, 211
Cook, William A., 42
Corse (Tennessee civilian), 178
Corsican soldier, 88
Courtney, Alfred R., 126
court-martial, 107–9, 239–40
cow in camp, 206, 248–54
cowardice, 139, 199
Cowardin, Charlie, 261
Craddock, R. B., 107
Crafton, John H., 48
Culpeper Court-house, Va., 76–77,
    91–93
Custer, George A., 217, 221–24

Dale (Tennessee woman), 178
Dalton, Ga., 155
Darden, James C., 43–44, 63–64,
    77–78, 89, 91, 162, 188–92,
    203, 211
Davis, Jefferson, 32, 78, 91, 161,
    171–72, 241
Dearing, James, 245–26
Denny, Thomas A., 179–80
deserters, 189–92, 211, 216–18
Dickinson, Bettie, 109–14
Dickinson, Samuel T., 109–11